The European project in collapse. Far from bringing prosperity and peace, the euro has catalysed an economic crisis and stirred up national antagonisms. We can now see clearly that the intellectual basis of European integration was false. Daniel Hannan, a Euro-MP and pro-European opponent of the Brussels system, exposes the design flaws in the EU and proposes a wholly different European dispensation: one based on the natural loyalties and affinities of the nation-state. As he argues in this powerful polemic, Britain is uniquely equipped by her temperament, her political system and her present position to catalyse this transformation.

Daniel Hannan is a writer and journalist, and has been Conservative MEP for South East England since 1999. He speaks French and Spanish and loves Europe, but believes that the European Union is making its constituent nations poorer, less democratic and less free.

Hannan was educated at Marlborough and Oriel College, Oxford. He worked as a speechwriter for William Hague and Michael Howard. He has been writing for the *Daily Telegraph* since 1996, and also contributes to numerous other publications including the *Wall Street Journal*, *The Times*, the *Washington Examiner*, *The Spectator*, *The Australian*, *The Catholic Herald*, *Die Welt* (Germany) and *Weltwoche* (Switzerland). He is the author of nine books, of which the most recent – *The New Road to Serfdom: A Letter of Warning to America* – is a *New York Times* bestseller. He blogs every day at www.hannan.co.uk, addressing political and cultural issues.

Daniel Hannan

—

A DOOMED MARRIAGE
Britain and Europe

 Notting Hill Editions

Published in 2012
by Notting Hill Editions Ltd
Newcombe House, 45 Notting Hill Gate
London W11 3LQ

Designed by FLOK Design, Berlin, Germany
Typeset by CB editions, London

Printed and bound
by Memminger MedienCentrum, Memmingen, Germany

A CIP record for this book
is available from the British Library
ISBN 978-1-907-90322-9

www.nottinghilleditions.com

Contents

– Introduction –

Permanence is the illusion of every age. When a ruling ideology loses its authority, it collapses more quickly than anyone had expected.

Think of the last major revolution in Europe: the *évènements* of 1989 that brought down the Communist regimes of the Warsaw Pact. In retrospect, it seems almost inevitable that such a false and decayed system should collapse in on itself; but almost no one thought so at the time.

During the 1980s, anti-Communist dissidents hoped for a gradual liberalisation that might unfold over a generation or more. Their sympathisers in the West were no more optimistic: in their most hopeful scenario, the technological superiority of the capitalist world would tell over several decades. The handful of eccentrics who predicted an earlier demise thought in terms of a violent catalyst: an exogenous shock, or perhaps a Chernobyl-style disaster. In the event, regime change was triggered by an almost trivial development: the decision by the Hungarian authorities no longer to require exit visas from East Germans wishing to visit Austria. Within days, Europe was convulsed in revolution, and free elections were being scheduled.

Change comes suddenly when the *ancien régime* loses its legitimacy. It came suddenly to King Louis XVI, to Tsar Nicholas II, to Shah Mohammad Reza Pahlavi. It came suddenly to the despots of North Africa. One moment, everything seems normal; the next, the statues of the former rulers are vast and trunkless legs of stone. In each case, downfall comes when the official version of reality is no longer compatible with people's experience.

The European Union is not, of course, an autocracy. Its own structures might be undemocratic, but its member nations are pluralist parliamentary regimes. Any country is free to leave the EU; any citizen to criticise Brussels; any politician to demand the repatriation of jurisdiction. Nonetheless, as in all pre-revolutionary moments, we see a chasm opening up between the official version of events and the reality.

EU institutions devote a great deal of time and money to promoting themselves. Millions of euros are spent on flying journalists, especially local journalists, to Brussels, and showing them a good time. Projects are promoted in the member states with an eye to maximising their publicity value to the EU, from highways to orchestras. There is even a department that specialises in material aimed at children, responsible for such unintentionally hilarious ventures as the *Captain Euro* cartoon books, in which an Aryan-looking federalist superhero battles an evil financier by the name of Dr D. Vider whose aim is to sunder Europe.

In its own account, the EU is an uncomplicated force for good in the world. It stands for peace, freedom and democracy – and, by implication, those who oppose it do not.

The trouble is that this EU exists only in a virtual world, a world of Commission press releases, Council communiqués and Parliamentary resolutions. In reality, the EU has an altogether more complicated relationship with liberal values. Abroad, it refuses to deal with the anti-Castro dissidents in Havana, it funnels money to Hamas, it declares its willingness to sell weapons to Beijing. At home, it swats aside referendum results when they go the 'wrong' way.

The EU can be remarkably intolerant of dissent. Commission employees found guilty of outright bribe-taking often escape with a demotion, but when a British official called Bernard Connolly criticised the euro, he was immediately thrown out. Money has been regularly siphoned off the EU budget without consequences for the perpetrators, but when the EU's chief accountant, Mara Andreasen, drew attention to flaws in the accounting system, she was dismissed. When a German reporter, Hans-Martin Tillack of *Stern* magazine, exposed organised looting in the EU's statistical office, Eurostat, it was he, rather than the accused fraudsters, who found himself arrested.

Malfeasance is not a peculiar property of the EU, of course. Man is fallen and, in any organisation, some individuals give in to temptation. What sets the EU aside is the discrepancy between its version of the truth and everyone else's. Warsaw Pact dissidents used to call it 'the gap between what is said and what is'. As long as this discrepancy was confined to the Brussels institutions, it didn't much matter to most Europeans. The euro crisis, however, has brought it into every home. The single currency turns out to have been sold on a fake premise. It was supposed to make citizens better off and to draw its member countries together. It has in practice, and wholly predictably, had the opposite effect. Suddenly, 'the gap between what is said and what is' has tangible economic consequences for most Europeans. Yet Brussels apparatchiks, not knowing what else to do, carry on canting their old slogans about peace and prosperity.

People are capable of extrapolating from the failure of the EU's most momentous project. On closer inspection, it turns out that the entire European proposition rests on empty slogans. It hasn't made its constituent nations wealthier. It hasn't been democratic. It hasn't entrenched the rule of law.

Even the initial impulse behind it – the sublimation of nationalism – has taken a rather bizarre form. While national sovereignty is indeed frowned on, Euro-nationalism – that is, the promotion of

the symbols of the EU and the projection of its per-
ceived collective interests in the world – has become
a substitute ideology.

Above all, the undertaking has lost its spirit. The
first generation of Euro-leaders were believers; their
successors are employees. In its early days, the EU
was run by idealists who truly thought that they were
bringing recovery and stability to a war-ravaged continent. While you can still find a few such individuals, they are nowadays vastly outnumbered by those
who have found, in the Euro-system, a way to make
a good living. The machine hums on, but the ghost
has departed.

As the economic downturn continues, voters are
coming to resent a system which, hitherto, they had
tolerated without giving the matter much thought.
When they see every euro their national governments save through domestic cuts being squandered
in the EU budget, they become angry. When they
read of Euro-officials flying about in private jets
while preaching austerity to the member states, they
suspect a racket.

The old incantations are losing their force. No
longer can criticism of such a system be dismissed as
xenophobia. I've lost count of how often I've been
told that, because I criticise the Brussels system, I am
anti-European. In fact I speak French and Spanish
and have lived and worked all over Europe. I believe
that European civilisation has made extraordinary

contributions to the happiness of mankind: personal freedom, the rule of law, representative government. It is precisely because the EU is so ready to abandon these precepts in pursuit of deeper integration that I oppose it. I oppose it as someone who is Francophile, Germanophile, Italophile, Hellenophile, Turcophile, Hispanophile, Lusophile – but not Europhile if, by Europhile, we mean wanting to shift more powers from elected national governments to Brussels institutions.

When change comes, it comes suddenly. Things which appeared solid turn out to be baseless. For half a century, the EU – or 'Europe', as it calls itself – has chanted its spells, mesmerising the political class of an entire continent. Now, the moment of disenchantment is at hand.

> Our revels now are ended. These our actors,
> As I foretold you, were all spirits and
> Are melted into air, into thin air.

Chapter 1

– The official history –

I n September 2010, while its 27 constituent states were struggling to cut their national budgets, the European Parliament allocated £112.5 million to a new museum in Brussels: the House of European History. MEPs brushed aside criticism of the cost, insisting that the project was necessary 'to cultivate the memory of European history and European unification'.

Politicians are often *un*interested in history, but rarely *dis*interested. Every state has its foundation myth, every polity its heroic legends. As a rule, the more insecure the regime, the tighter it clutches at its approved narrative.

The EU's semi-authorised version of history goes something like this. Ever since the break-up of Charlemagne's imperium, if not since the fall of Rome, Europe has been weakened by its divisions. A continent which shared a common cultural and religious heritage was shattered into a hundred squabbling princedoms. These statelets wasted their energies on endless wars.

As technology developed, the states became more powerful and the wars more destructive. At some stage in the Early Modern period, a terrifying new ingredient was introduced: nationalism. No longer were conflicts largely professional affairs, conducted by kings and their hirelings. From now on, whole populations would be dragged – or, worse, would rush enthusiastically – into murderous battles.

Between 1914 and 1945, nationalism and war reached their climax. Fifty million Europeans died in the continent's last two great 'civil wars'. At which point, the survivors decided they had had enough. Since nation-states were the cause of war, their dissolution would be the means to peace. France and Germany had been fighting each other on and off ever since they came into being at the dissolution of the Carolingian empire in 843. If they were merged again, the problem would be solved. Charles de Gaulle was later to describe the process of European integration as 'a revival of the whole concept of Charlemagne'.[1]

At this moment, the story continues, some visionary Europeans stepped forward. They were not soldiers or statesmen of the old school. Europe had had enough of that. Some were elected politicians, others technocrats. All, though, saw their mandate as coming from their understanding of what needed to be done. There is no formal list of Europe's founding fathers, but seven men are recognised in almost every tally: Konrad Adenauer, Jean Monnet, Paul-Henri Spaak, Alcide De Gasperi, Robert Schuman, Joseph Bech and Johan Willem Beyen.

These men had something in common which is rarely if ever remarked. All except Jean Monnet (who was from Cognac) came from the Carolingian heartland. Spaak, Bech and Beyen were, respectively, from the three Benelux states. The Italian, Alcide De Gasperi, was from the Tyrol, which was Austrian at the time of his birth. The German, Konrad Adenauer, was from Cologne, close to Charlemagne's capital at Aachen. The Frenchman, Robert Schuman, the man now hailed as the father of the EU, was from Lorraine, which was part of Germany when he was born; his mother was Luxembourgish.

These patriarchs, runs Europe's official history, transcended nationalism and united Europe in peace. The pooling of Europe's resources made war impractical, and the pooling of sovereignty made it unthinkable.

As Europeans fell into the habit of working together, it became hard to imagine that they would ever again vote for extremists or chauvinists. The European model proved attractive: three more countries joined in 1973, a further three by 1986, three more in 1995, ten in 2004 and two in 2007.

Europe spread its values, according to its apologists, not with bombs, but with trade accords. Its greatest threat to a neighbouring country was not to invade it, but to ignore it. The prospect of European co-operation encouraged applicant nations to adopt more liberal domestic policies. Poland softened her abortion laws, Croatia handed over her war criminals, Turkey eased restrictions on her minorities.

More and more countries opted voluntarily to belong. Europe's mixed-market model – neither so harsh as American capitalism nor so authoritarian as Soviet Communism – proved irresistible. Other parts of the world began to form themselves into regional blocs in mimicry of the EU: ASEAN, Mercosur, the African Union and so on. These associations were, indeed, initially sponsored by Brussels, which continues to bolster them by refusing to sign trade or aid accords with individual states, instead insisting on 'bloc-to-bloc' deals.

As more and more countries are drawn into the Eurosphere, the tale concludes, and as aggressive patriotism recedes across the world, we are approaching something like the end of history. At any rate, the nationalist demons that have tormented humanity through the centuries are at last being exorcised.

That, as I say, is the official version and, like all official versions, it contains specks of truth. Certainly, its core element – the belief that European integration is an antidote to nationalism and war – is sincerely believed by most supporters of the project. Nonetheless, every aspect of this narrative needs qualification, starting with the premise that the break-up of empires into smaller units is bad for progress. All the evidence suggests that the opposite is true.

Europe's rise to global hegemony came at a time when, unlike the great civilisations of Asia, it was politically disunited. Five hundred years ago, the Oriental dynasties – the Mings in China, the Moguls in India, the Ottomans in the Near and Middle East – held a clear technological lead over the scattered peoples at the western tip of the Eurasian landmass. European visitors to the Eastern courts marvelled at what they saw: gunpowder, paper money, canals, advanced mathematics, medicine, astronomy and cartography. It would have seemed a safe bet that the Asian powers would dominate Europe for the rest of the millennium, that the Chinese would sail around Africa to plant trade missions in Portugal rather than the other way around.

In fact, Europe's disunity turned out to be its strength. The Oriental monarchies, being unitary states, became uniform, regulated and highly taxed. Innovation was stifled, and bureaucracy burgeoned. But Europe never became a single state. Instead, its constituent entities jostled and strove to outdo each other. New ideas could be tried in one place and, if successful, copied in others. As Paul Kennedy showed in *The Rise and Fall of the Great Powers*, such diversity encouraged enterprise and risk-taking. Just as competition among individuals tends to boost growth, so does competition among states.[2]

One of the saddest aspects of European integration is that the current EU mandarinate – the appellation is unusually apposite in this context – is determined to go down the Ming-Mogul-Ottoman route to harmonisation at the very moment that the great nations of Asia have discovered the virtues of devolution and decentralisation. In the name of Europe, Eurocrats have undone the secret of Europe's success: the diversity, variety and pluralism that raised their continent to greatness.

There were some critics who saw this clearly at the outset. The renowned liberal economist Wilhelm Röpke, who had been one of the first Germans to apprehend the Nazi menace, grasped right away that the ambitions of the Euro-patriarchs would jeopardise Europe's cultural success. In 1960, as France, Germany and the Benelux states made their first tentative steps toward integration, he made a perceptive observation:

In antiquity, Strabo spoke of the 'many shapes' of Europe; Montesquieu would speak of Europe as a 'nation de nations'; in our own time Christopher Dawson has stressed Europe's character of a 'society of peoples'. Decentrism is of the essence of the spirit of Europe. To try to organise Europe centrally, to subject the Continent to a bureaucracy of economic planning, to weld it into a bloc, would be nothing less than a betrayal of Europe and the European patrimony. The betrayal would be the more perfidious for being perpetrated in the name of Europe and by an outrageous misuse of that name.[3]

The notion that size is a precondition of prosperity is belied by the facts. If it were true, China would be wealthier than Hong Kong, Indonesia than Brunei – the EU itself, for that matter, than Switzerland. All the evidence suggests that the opposite is the case: that states flourish economically when decisions are taken as closely as possible to the people they affect.

The table overleaf shows where the wealthiest people in the world live. Eighteen of the top twenty countries have small – in some cases, very small – populations. Australia just makes it into the list. But the big exception (in both senses) is the United States. How did the US manage to creep up the scale alongside all the micro-states? Because, with the exception of Switzerland, it is the most decentralised polity on Earth, governing itself like a coalition of statelets. In some senses, the 50 states of the US enjoy more sovereignty than nations within the EU, on issues ranging from indirect taxation to capital punishment.

What, though, of the contention that political unity secures peace and freedom? This, for most Euro-integrationists, was the greater consideration. Their speeches and writings were focused on the political, rather than the economic, virtues of amalgamation. Though they rarely put it in these terms, they would have seen a decline in economic growth as a price worth paying for unity. War, they might have added, was far more deleterious to wealth creation than anything else.

SMALL IS BEAUTIFUL[4]
[GDP per capita]

1	Liechtenstein	$ 141,100	(2008 est.)
2	Qatar	$ 102,700	(2011 est.)
3	Luxembourg	$ 84,700	(2011 est.)
4	Bermuda	$ 69,900	(2004 est.)
5	Singapore	$ 59,900	(2011 est.)
6	Jersey	$ 57,000	(2005 est.)
7	Falkland Islands	$ 55,400	(2002 est.)
8	Norway	$ 53,300	(2011 est.)
9	Brunei	$ 49,400	(2011 est.)
10	Hong Kong	$ 49,300	(2011 est.)
11	United Arab Emirates	$ 48,500	(2011 est.)
12	United States	$ 48,100	(2011 est.)
13	Guernsey	$ 44,600	(2005 est.)
14	Cayman Islands	$ 43,800	(2004 est.)
15	Switzerland	$ 43,400	(2011 est.)
16	Gibraltar	$ 43,000	(2006 est.)
17	Netherlands	$ 42,300	(2011 est.)
18	Austria	$ 41,700	(2011 est.)
19	Australia	$ 40,800	(2011 est.)
20	Kuwait	$ 40,700	(2011 est.)

Yet the notion that large political units are more peaceful or more liberal than small ones is easier to uphold in theory than in practice.

Stability, though an end itself for many diplomats, is an overrated virtue. A tyranny can be a remarkably stable entity; and while stability is generally in the interests of the tyrant, it is rarely in the interest of his subjects. The Soviet Union was the largest multinational state of modern times and, while it was certainly stable, it was a wretched place to live.

To this day, Euro-diplomats tend to place great emphasis on steadiness; more so, in many instances, than on freedom. Think of the international questions on which the US and EU diplomatic machines fundamentally differ – whether to deal with the anti-Castro resistance in Cuba, whether to engage with the ayatollahs in Tehran, whether to back Taiwan – and you will descry a pattern. The Brussels official is keener than his State Department counterpart to work with what he finds, to deal with existing rulers, to encourage reform rather than seek regime change. The European Union, born out of a reaction against disunity and war, favours stability over democracy. The United States, born out of a popular revolt against a remote regime, reverses those priorities.

Stability, almost by definition, suits the people in charge. It is therefore the justification of every dictatorship: *après moi, le déluge*. Such a plea is perhaps likelier to resonate with the Euro-functionary, himself the product of an essentially undemocratic system, than with an elected representative.

Yet there is no intrinsic virtue in a large, stable state – especially when its size and stability are purchased at the expense of freedom. This point was beautifully made by Edward Gibbon, a Europhile by almost any contemporary standard, and a nostalgist for the Roman Empire whose collapse he chronicled. Gibbon saw advantages in political unity, and argued that the best time to have been alive was the second century AD, between the death of the emperor Domitian and the accession of Commodus. Yet he also recognised that the advantages of peace and stability were outweighed by the dangers inherent in pan-continental rule:

The division of Europe into a number of independent states, connected, however, with each other by the general resemblance of religion, language, and manners, is productive of the most beneficial consequences to the liberty of mankind. A modern tyrant, who should find no resistance either in his own breast, or in his people, would soon experience a gentle restraint from the example of his equals, the dread of present censure, the advice of his allies and the apprehension of his enemies. The object of his displeasure, escaping from the narrow limits of his dominions, would easily obtain, in a happier climate, a secure refuge, a new fortune adequate to his merit, the freedom of complaint and, perhaps, the means of revenge.[5]

Gibbon was well aware of the vital importance of political asylum. He understood that driving people into exile tended to debilitate the tyranny from which they were banished and strengthen the land that received them. To pluck one example from the many with which he was familiar, France expelled her Protestant population with the Revocation of the Edict of Nantes in 1685. At a stroke, Louis XIV lost 400,000 of his most enterprising subjects. The refugees fled to Great Britain, Switzerland, North America, South Africa and the Low Countries and, in so doing, tipped the balance of power permanently and comprehensively against the power that had ejected them.

Britain was in a state of intermittent conflict with France between 1689 and 1815. On paper, France had all the advantages: a greater territory, richer resources and a population nearly four times the size of her rival's. Yet Britain emerged ultimately victorious because she made up in enterprise what she lacked in territorial advantages. In particular, she developed modern capital markets, allowing her to concentrate resources in a way that the French never could. That process owed a great deal to the Huguenot exiles, whose energy would otherwise have been placed at the disposal of the Bourbons.

The phenomenon of the enterprising asylum-seeker has been observed many times since, the outstanding example perhaps being the intellectual contribution made to the Allied cause by Jews who had been forced to flee fascist Europe.

Which brings us neatly to the single greatest dissonance in the EU-approved version of history, namely the conviction that European integration was and is an antidote to the horrors of Nazism.

From the beginning, this has been the backstop

of every integrationist argument. All right, the CAP might be wasteful, but surely it's a price worth paying for peace! True, the budget might not have been approved for eighteen years, but at least there are no more fascist demagogues! You don't like the lack of democracy in Brussels? Would you rather have a second Holocaust?

This last argument was made quite blatantly by the then Swedish Commissioner, Margot Wallström, in the run-up to the French and Dutch plebiscites on the European Constitution in 2005. Attending a ceremony to mark the anniversary of the liberation of the Terezin ghetto in the Czech Republic, she warned that 'No' votes in the coming referendums might lead to another genocide:

There are those today who want to scrap the supra-national idea. They want the EU to go back to the old purely inter-governmental way of doing things. I say those people should come to Terezin and see where that old road leads.[6]

There are several objections to be made to this thesis (beyond the obvious one that it turned out to be false: France and the Netherlands both voted 'No', yet there has been no Nazi revival). Most strikingly, any ideology that presents itself as the sole alternative to fascism is allowing itself a great deal of leeway. After all, if European integration were the only thing that stood in the way of war and genocide, it could get away with being remarkably illiberal and undemocratic while yet remaining the better option.

I don't make this point glibly. In the thirteen years I have spent as an MEP, I have heard the excuse trotted out again and again. When a Euro-federalist is confronted with some monstrous failing of the Brussels system, one which he feels unable to justify, he will almost invariably say: 'OK, OK, but at least it's better than nationalism.'

It's not a new tactic. The Stalinist regimes of the Comecon states initially called themselves Anti-Fascist Fronts. Their leaders, like many contemporary Eurocrats, half-believed their own propaganda. In their own eyes, at least, they had earned some sort of mandate through their active resistance to Hitler. While others had collaborated, they, the small cadre of Communists, had been imprisoned for their beliefs, or had waged partisan guerrilla campaigns. The conviction that Communism was the practical alternative to fascism formed the basis, in private at any rate, of their sense of legitimacy. In Czechoslovakia, Yugoslavia and the GDR, at least in the early days, it was also a public justification.

As an aside, it is interesting to note that, despite their later adoption of the anti-Nazi cause, few of the early Euro-leaders had had especially glorious war records. A handful, notably the Italian Christian Democrat, Alcide De Gasperi, had actively opposed fascism. A few more, such as François Mitterand, had actively collaborated. Most had simply kept their heads down. In his seminal study *The Tainted Source*, John Laughland showed that the Euro-patriarchs had been keener than the population at large on working with fascist and Quisling regimes.[7]

Of course, those who have never had to live through a military occupation should not rush to judgement. There is no suggestion that the antifascism of the Euro-patriarchs was insincere. On the contrary, they were plainly genuine in their conviction that they were burying the horrors through which they had recently passed.

Harder to shake off, perhaps, is the way in which the 'Europeanist' propaganda employed by the Nazis and their allies continued into the 1950s, albeit in an adjusted and democratic form. Both at an intellectual and a popular level, fascist regimes in the early 1940s had justified themselves by positing a European identity. Europe, they argued, was a haven of civilisation between two forms of barbarism: the Anglo-Saxon savagery of unregulated markets and crass commercialism, and the Soviet savagery of total communism. That argument has never entirely gone away.

Ideas are not responsible, of course, for the people who take them up. I mention this coincidence of imagery simply to contextualise the assertion that European integration is an antidote to Nazism. Before making a claim of such magnitude,

Euro-enthusiasts should be absolutely certain of their moral right to do so.

To repeat, modern Europhiles are unquestionably sincere in their dislike of Nazism. Nothing is more misplaced than the suggestion, which one occasionally hears all over Europe, that the EU is really some sort of continuation of German expansionism. Quite apart from being terrifically rude, the charge is the opposite of the truth. Far from harbouring secret imperial ambitions, most modern Germans suffer from a lack of patriotism that borders almost on self-abnegation.

The reason that John Laughland's work is worth citing is that, having made such an issue out of their anti-Nazi credentials, supporters of the European project invite an evaluation of that argument. I'd much rather not be discussing the issue at all – references to the Second World War in modern politics should be entered into, as the Prayer Book says of matrimony, reverently, discreetly, advisedly, soberly. But, by constantly arguing that the EU is the only reason we have enjoyed peace since 1945, the integrationists more or less oblige us to address the question. Here, for example is Herman Van Rompuy, the EU President:

We have together to fight the danger of a new Euroscepticism. The biggest enemy of Europe today is fear. Fear leads to egoism, egoism leads to nationalism, and nationalism leads to war.[8]

Here is the German Chancellor, Angela Merkel:

Nobody should believe that another half century of peace in
Europe is a given – it's not. So I say again: if the euro collapses, Europe collapses. That can't happen.[9]

Since we have been forced into this distasteful
debate, let's at least be accurate. Was the EU a *cause*
of European peace, or was it rather a *consequence* of
the peace brought about by the defeat of fascism, the
spread of democracy and the Nato alliance? Is it a
vaccine against Nazism, or simply the latest in a long
line of presumptuous supra-national ideologies?

The notion that, as Herman Van Rompuy puts
it, 'nationalism leads to war' is more often asserted
than explained. Looking back over the past half
millennium, we find plenty of wars that have ideological rather than national roots. Europe was, for
example, more often plunged into conflict by religious than by national differences. The wars of the
Counter-Reformation were not patriotic conflicts.
From Münster to Drogheda, terrible atrocities were
committed by men of the same blood and speech.
The Thirty Years War (1618–48) was the longest
continuous war in Europe's history and, on some
measures, proportionately the most lethal, yet it di-
vided people by faith, not nationality. As the ever-
wise historian Lord Macaulay wryly observed:

The experience of many ages teaches us that men may be

ready to fight to the death, and to persecute without pity, for a religion whose creed they do not understand, and whose precepts they habitually disobey.[10]

More recently, political differences came to replace religious ones, generating the same fanaticism in twentieth-century men that sectarianism had been capable of generating in their great-grandparents. Fascism and Communism were to cause far more death and destruction than any nationalist conflicts. It's true, of course, that, as with any wars, national interests became entangled with the doctrinal schisms. The Second World War and the Cold War were not simply ideological clashes; they also ranged whole countries against each other. But they were *primarily* ideological wars, which cut across national differences.

This was obviously true of the Cold War, but it was true, too, of the Nazi aggression. There wasn't a country in Europe which didn't have combatants on both sides. When Berlin fell in 1945, the last troops still standing in its defence were the Scandinavian and French soldiers of, respectively, the Nordica and Charlemagne Waffen-SS regiments (both of which, incidentally, had sought recruits on grounds of 'defending Europe').[11]

Where nationalism *was* at the root of a conflict, it was usually nationalism of a people who had been, as it were, incorporated into the wrong state. The nineteenth century saw several wars which began as risings against foreign rule, or as attempts to embrace *irredenti* populations. When Euro-enthusiasts blame the two world wars on 'nationalism', they rarely emphasise what *kind* of nationalism it was. The Great War was sparked by the demand of the South Slav citizens of Austria-Hungary for statehood; the Second World War by Hitler's annexation of German-speaking parts of Poland. It's true, of course, that these were by no means the only causes of their respective conflagrations. Still, the point is worth emphasising. Look around the world today, and see how many conflicts are rooted in the misalignment of state borders with national affinities. It is hard to find much basis for the contention that jamming different nationalities together makes them less rather than more antagonistic.

As for the Wallström/Terezin line of reasoning, if we absolutely must drag the Holocaust into the argument, it is worth stressing that national citizenship was, for many European Jews and other victims, their only defence against the murderers. In his chilling, because matter-of-fact, chronicle of the killings, Robert Wistricht noted that even fascist and collaborationist regimes tended to draw a distinction between their own nationals and refugees who had fled to their territory. Most Axis and occupied governments recognised an obligation to their Jewish citizens which (with the exception of Denmark and the partial exception of Bulgaria) they refused to extend to foreign nationals who had entered their jurisdiction as the result of persecution elsewhere. The Nazis well understood this tendency, which was why one of their first acts, on seizing control of a new territory, was to declare all Jews stateless.[12] The worst massacres took place in those parts of Europe where there was nothing resembling a national government, namely the Nazi-occupied parts of Poland, Lithuania and the USSR. The Jewish inhabitants of these territories were statistically far less likely to survive the war than those in the Third Reich itself.

I make this point not simply for the sake of challenging Mrs Wallström's interpretation of history, but to draw attention to the role of the nation-state as a defender of liberty. Over the years, national units have proved remarkably secure vessels of freedom. One after another, various 'isms' have arisen which purport to be bigger than the nation-state: fascism, Marxism, Islamic fundamentalism. In each case, their very presumption, their refusal to recognise accepted notions of state sovereignty or territorial jurisdiction, makes them volatile. And in each case, nation-states, rooted as they are in genuine affinities, have been bulwarks against them.

The Iranian Revolution, like the French and the Russian, regarded itself as bigger than the nation-state. Its signature act was the siege of the US embassy: a shocking violation of all accepted norms of international law. Even during the Second World War, when mutually opposed ideologies strove to extirpate each other, diplomats were peaceably evacuated through neutral states. In signalling their disregard for national sovereignty, the ayatollahs were announcing that their legitimacy came from a source higher than the recognised law of nations. That is always a dangerous conceit and, like the Bolsheviks before them, they immediately sought to replicate their revolution around the world, sponsoring militias from the Balkans to Central Asia, striking as far afield as London and Buenos Aires.

The nation-state, with all its imperfections, was and is a bulwark against ideologies which spill out violently from behind national borders. Precisely because nation-states have grown organically, and are rooted in a degree of popular consent, they have a natural bias against belligerent and revolutionary doctrines. The idea that nationalism is an unstable or dangerous force is, indeed, a remarkably new one.

During the Second World War, a constant theme of Churchill's rhetoric, and of Allied propaganda more generally, was that Britain was fighting for the cause of all nations. Patriotism was not simply the focus of Britain's resistance to tyranny; it extended also to a respect for the freedom of friendly peoples. Britain had declared war in the first place in 1939 (as she had in 1914) because of the violation of the sovereignty of another country. Again and again, in their war aims and in their broadcasts to occupied Europe, the Allies stressed that they were fighting to restore the independence of nation-states throughout Europe.

This difference in perception partly explains why the United Kingdom was reluctant to involve itself in the first moves towards European federalism in the 1950s. British people did not share the sense that the nation-state had failed, or that patriotism was dangerous. They understood from their recent experience that, far from denigrating other countries, a genuine patriot values the freedom of all peoples.

As the Second World War recedes from memory, Europeans can take a more measured view of national loyalties. The reflexive equation of nationalism with chauvinism and war, which predominated in the 1950s, can now be placed in context. It is time, in short, to examine the case for the nation-state.

Chapter 2

– The case for nationalism –

When a *bien pensant* Europhile wishes to signal his strongest possible disapproval of something, he will use one of two words: 'nationalist' or 'populist'. Both epithets have become somewhat detached from their literal definitions. To adapt George Orwell on the word 'fascist', they have now little meaning except in so far as they signify 'something not desirable'.[1]

It is nonetheless interesting to see the two words so often yoked together, for they both carry a democratic implication. Any referendum that results in a rejection of closer European integration (which is to say, almost every referendum on the subject) is dismissed as both nationalist and populist. Any politician who accepts the result of such a poll is given both soubriquets in an especially bellicose tone.

They are indeed linked concepts. As Charles de Gaulle put it in 1942:

La démocratie se confond exactement, pour moi, avec la souveraineté nationale. La démocratie c'est le gouvernement du peuple par le peuple, et la souveraineté nationale, c'est le peuple exerçant sa souveraineté sans entrave.[2]

Nowadays, that notion sounds a little archaic; but in 1942, it would have seemed obvious. Democracy in its modern form had always been linked to the national principle. When radicals in the eighteenth and nineteenth centuries began to argue for one-man-one-vote, they almost invariably found themselves challenging the multinational units that existed across Europe. Having posited the revolutionary idea that government should be carried out by and for the people, they found that they had immediately raised another question: what people? Within what unit, in other words, were these democratic arguments to be played out?

That question had only one possible answer, and the democrats found it at once. Representative government, they argued, would work best within a population whose members felt enough in common one with another to accept government from each other's hands: in other words, within a nation. As the Italian patriot Giuseppe Mazzini put it, in perhaps the pithiest ever statement of the case for self-determination: 'Where there is a nation, let there be a state.'

A community of identity might rest on many things: history, geography, culture or religion. Language is the most common basis for nationhood, but there are exceptions. A strong sense of national identity can exist in a multilingual territory (Switzerland, for example); conversely, a monolingual population might contain more than one national identity (as among the Serbo-Croat speakers of the former Yugoslavia).

It is important to stress that these things are rarely straightforward. People are capable of sustaining more than one identity: you might feel Scottish as well as British, Corsican as well as French. Identities can mutate over time. An arbitrary political frontier might, as the decades pass, become a genuine national one (something of the sort has happened between Austria and Southern Germany, and across much of South America). And, of course, languages themselves are political. When, following devolution, Irish was recognised as an official language in Northern Ireland (despite not being the native tongue of anyone born there), Unionists responded by granting equal status to 'Ulster Scots' – which until then had been generally considered a patois. As the Yiddish linguist Max Weinreich observed, 'a language is a dialect with an army and navy'.[3]

None of these complications, though, compromises the essential principle. A polity functions best when there is a sense of shared identity. That sense, being visceral, might defy logical definition; but it is no less real for that.

Multinational democracies are rarely stable. By multinational, I don't mean a society which is in the process of assimilating minorities, nor yet one with small foreign populations. Virtually every state in the world has some minorities, if only as the result of immigration. I am talking here of states where large and settled communities have different loyalties. Many such states have existed through history, but they have rarely been democratic. Indeed, the rule is that, once their peoples are given the vote, they opt for separation. The Soviet and Yugoslav federations went the same way as the Ottoman and Habsburg empires: their constituent peoples couldn't be held together once they were free to choose.

To repeat, these things are rarely clear-cut. A multinational democracy can unravel slowly and peacefully, as Belgium has been doing for decades. It can tolerate a measure of continuing secessionist discontent without ceasing to be democratic, as India does. And, of course, not all separatist feelings are of equal intensity. Look at two examples, one from either end of the spectrum. The world's newest state, South Sudan, was different in almost every way from the rest of Sudan: ethnically, religiously, linguistically. It had been through a secessionist war, and eventually broke away in rancour and enmity. No one, by contrast, has ever fired a shot in anger over the issue of Scottish secession. Indeed, it is far from clear that Scottish identity is of the kind that generally constitutes national separateness. On most of the usual denominators, Scotland forms part of the same national continuum as the rest of the United Kingdom. Scots watch the same television programmes, follow the same sports, eat the same food, shop at the same chains and speak the same language as people elsewhere in Britain. As the aboriginal Unionist, James VI & I, put it:

Hath not God first united these Kingdoms, both in Language and in Religion and in Similitude of Manners? Yea, hath He not made us all in one Island, compassed by one Sea, and of itself by Nature so indivisible, as almost those that were Borderers themselves on the late Borders, cannot distinguish nor know or discern their own limits?[4]

Opinion polls in Scotland suggest that the issue of independence turns mainly on the economics. A survey by Scottish Social Attitudes in December 2011 found that, if separation would make them £500 a year better off, Scots would back it by 65 per cent to 25; told that it would make them £500 a year worse off, only 21 per cent supported it, with 66 per cent opposed. It is hard to believe that any such considerations would have swayed the people of South Sudan, who voted by 98 per cent in a referendum for secession. Unlike Scots, they were in no doubt that they constituted a wholly separate race.

For all these shades of grey, the principle holds. Other things being equal, our inclination should be to allow people to determine their own borders. Or, to put it another way, the most important consideration when determining national frontiers should be the wishes of the inhabitants. This is not to say that alternative claims – geography, history, past treaties, rights of the residual state to access – have no force; simply that they ought not to override the claim of self-determination.

This point is worth emphasising because, at present, our ruling ideology is based on precisely the opposite principle. International organisations – naturally enough, you might say – actively *oppose* the national principle. The UN and the EU, in particular, hold up the multinational state as a desirable end in itself, and are prepared to invest considerable resources in ensuring that state borders don't coincide with ethnographic ones.

This is most obvious in the case of the two European territories that the international community administers as protectorates: Bosnia-Herzegovina and Kosovo. The former is run by an EU-appointed High Representative, the latter by a UN-approved general. In both cases, the primary purpose of such rule is to prevent a readjustment of borders along the lines that local people favour.

In neither case is the territorial integrity of the state based on a fear of ethnic cleansing. On the contrary, the Serbs of both territories are now clustered conveniently close to Serbia proper. In the case of Kosovo, the *de facto* border is already the ethnographic one. But to regularise this line would mean accepting the validity of national self-determination as a concept – which would, of course, destroy the intellectual foundations of the entire European project. As Upton Sinclair used to observe, it is remarkably difficult to make a man understand something when his salary depends upon his not understanding it.

And so, in pursuit of multinationalism, democracy is vitiated. Dozens of elected officials have been dismissed in Bosnia-Herzegovina for, in effect, failing to uphold the EU's approved orthodoxy of multinationalism. Both states have adopted variants of the EU flag – stars on a blue background – so as to emphasise their post-national nature. Kosovo's first national anthem was the EU's own 'Ode to Joy'. When it eventually wrote its own, it plumped for a wordless tune called 'Europe'.

In other words, the EU is exporting its ideology, just as it does when seeking to force non-European states into their own regional unions. It is determined to ensure that neighbouring countries form political units based on something other than the national principle. Why? Because European construction itself rests on the doctrine that national loyalties are arbitrary, transient and discreditable. When it bars the election of nationalist politicians in its satrapies, it is simply extending the principle that leads it to disallow 'no' votes in referendums within its own borders. De Gaulle was right to say that democracy and national self-determination are the same thing. Deny the second and, pretty soon, you find yourself having to deny the first.

While on the subject of the Balkans, it's worth dealing with one of the more common objections to the right of self-determination, namely the idea that partition is invariably a wretched and violent experience. It can be, of course. Any change in political borders is potentially disruptive. In British India, partition resulted in terror and bloodshed, and in repeated wars between India and Pakistan. In Ireland (or, strictly speaking, in the United Kingdom, which was the entity partitioned in 1921), there were civil wars on both sides of the new frontier: a short and intense one to the south, a protracted and intermittent one to the north.

In both cases, though, it can at least be argued that these problems were greatly exacerbated by a failure properly to apply the national principle. The treaty which established Northern Ireland also provided for a Boundary Commission to redraw the border. It met between 1922 and 1925 and duly recommended substantial changes: the Irish Free State would have gained most of South Armagh and Co. Londonderry, and ceded a chunk of Co. Donegal, along with some other minor adjustments. Had these alterations been implemented, much subsequent anguish might have been averted.

In India, the failure was even greater: more Muslims were stranded in India than incorporated into Pakistan, and parts of the border bore no relation whatever to local preferences. These regions – above all, Kashmir, whose promised plebiscite was never held – have been in a state of semi-permanent conflict ever since, serving to poison relations between Pakistan and India.

In any case, it is misleading to hold up the worst cases as typical. There are plenty of examples of peaceful divorces: Czechoslovakia, the West Indies Federation, Serbia-Montenegro. It's true that the interspersing of populations can be a complicating factor. Yugoslavia is often cited as a textbook example of why partition is wrong, and the EU's determination to maintain the territorial integrity of Bosnia-Herzegovina is sometimes justified as an attempt to prevent a repeat of the horrors of the early 1990s. In fact, the way to have avoided those horrors would have been through a series of plebiscites, overseen by neutral observers. The resulting borders would have been almost exactly what they are now – with the difference that it might not have been necessary to fight a series of monstrous wars to secure them.

Had the international community accepted the case for national self-determination at the outset, and offered to mediate a series of votes and, where necessary, voluntary population exchanges, we might have been spared the horrors of war and ethnic cleansing. Instead, when Slovenia, in a referendum held on 23 December 1990, became the first state to declare independence, following a referendum in which 94.8 per cent of those taking part (and an extraordinary 88.5 per cent of all eligible voters) opted for secession, the EU responded by insisting on 'the territorial integrity of the Yugoslav federation'. It announced that any states which withdrew from the federation would be denied trade and aid accords. Only when the war had utterly destroyed the old state did it reluctantly recognise the reality of Croatian and Slovenian independence.[5]

The EU's distrust of the nation-state is perhaps most obvious in its relations with Israel. No country in the world so clearly embodies the national principle. For 2,000 years, Jews were scattered and stateless, but never lost their aspiration to statehood: 'Next year in Jerusalem.' If Israel's claim is valid – if people are truly better off living in their own national groups – then everything the EU has done since its foundation in 1956 is questionable. Which is why, in recent years, Brussels has shifted from a more or less uncomplicatedly pro-Palestinian position (the EU has long been the chief financial sponsor of the Palestinian entity in its various forms) to calling for regional integration and a dismantling of barriers – a process which, of course, poses a far more existential threat to the Jewish state. Israelis sometimes blame this attitude on anti-Americanism, or anti-Semitism. In fact, the EU is being perfectly consistent, rejecting national claims abroad as it does within its own territory.

In order to sustain the imperatives of integration, the EU is not only undemocratic in itself; it also requires its member nations to surrender a measure of their domestic accountability. As we shall now see, Charles de Gaulle was right in more ways than he knew.

Chapter 3

– Why the EU can't be democratic –

D emocracy is not simply a periodic right to mark a cross on a ballot paper. It also depends upon a relationship between government and governed, on a sense of common affinity and allegiance. To put it another way, democracy requires a *demos*: a unit with which we identify when we use the word 'we'. Take away the *demos* and you are left only with the *kratos*: the power of a state that must compel by force of law what it cannot ask in the name of civic patriotism.

In the absence of a *demos*, governments are even likelier than usual to purchase votes through, for example, public works schemes and sinecures. Lacking any natural, patriotic loyalty, they have to buy the support of their electorates. One way to think of the EU is as a massive vehicle for the redistribution of wealth. Taxpayers in all the states contribute (though their contributions are hidden among the national tax-takes), and the revenue is then used to purchase the allegiance of articulate and powerful groups: consultants, contractors, big landowners, NGOs, corporations, charities, municipalities.

Unsurprisingly, the people running the EU have

little time for the concept of representative government. The (unelected) President of the European Commission, José Manuel Durão Barroso, argues that nation-states are dangerous precisely because they are excessively democratic:

Governments are not always right. If governments were always right we would not have the situation that we have today. Decisions taken by the most democratic institutions in the world are very often wrong.[1]

This is, of course, a reaffirmation of de Gaulle's remark about democracy and national sovereignty being the same thing; the difference being that Mr Barroso sees both concepts as undesirable.

Which brings us to the gravamen of the case against the EU. It is contemptuous of public opinion, not by some oversight, but as an ineluctable consequence of its supra-national nature. There is an old joke in Brussels to the effect that, if the EU were a country applying to join itself, it would be rejected on grounds of being insufficiently democratic. The joke understates the magnitude of the problem.

The EU is run, extraordinarily, by a body that combines legislative and executive power. The European Commission is not only the EU's 'government'; it is also, in most fields of policy, the only body that can propose legislation. Such a concentration of power is itself objectionable enough; but what is truly extraordinary is that the 27 Commissioners are unelected. Many supporters of the EU acknowledge this flaw. They call it the EU's 'democratic deficit', and vaguely admit that something ought to be done about it. But the democratic deficit isn't an accidental design flaw; it is intrinsic to the whole project.

As we have seen, the EU's founding fathers had had a mixed experience with democracy – especially the populist and plebiscitary strain that came into vogue between the wars. Too much democracy was associated, in their minds, with demagoguery and fascism. There were, of course, differences of emphasis among them. The scheming Jean Monnet, who was never elected to public office, was more suspicious of the ballot box than his ascetic countryman Robert Schuman, who was twice prime minister of France. None the less, it is fair to say that the patriarchs prided themselves on creating a model where supreme power would be in the hands of 'experts': disinterested technocrats immune to the ballot box. They understood very well that a scheme as audacious as theirs, the merging of ancient kingdoms and republics into a single state, would never succeed if each successive transfer of power from the national capitals to Brussels had to be approved by the voters. They were therefore quite unapologetic about designing a system in which public opinion would be tempered or moderated by a bureau of wise men.

The EU's diffidence about representative government continues to this day, though it is not always articulated so blatantly as it was by Commissioner Barroso. When, for example, referendums go the 'wrong' way, Eurocrats think nothing of swatting the results aside. When Denmark voted against the Maastricht Treaty in 1992, Ireland against the Nice Treaty in 2001 and Ireland (again) against the Lisbon Treaty in 2008, people were told to go away and try again. When France and the Netherlands voted against the European Constitution in 2005, the verdict was simply disregarded.

I well remember the aftermath of those last two votes. One after another, MEPs and Eurocrats rose to explain that people hadn't really been voting against the European Constitution at all. They had actually been voting against Turkish accession, or Anglo-Saxon capitalism, or Jacques Chirac – anything, in fact, except the proposition actually on the ballot paper. As Jean-Claude Juncker, the Prime Minister of Luxembourg, explained: 'the French and Dutch did not really vote "No" to the European Constitution'.[2]

As in any abusive relationship, the contemptuous way in which Eurocrats treat voters has become self-reinforcing on both sides. The more voters are ignored, the more cynical and fatalistic they become. They abstain in record numbers, complaining – quite understandably – that it makes no difference how they cast their ballots. Eurocrats, for their part, are obliged to construct a world view that justifies their readiness to defy the verdict of the urns. They fall quickly into the habit of treating public opinion as an obstacle to overcome rather than a reason to change direction. The imperatives of European integration require them to disregard popular majorities on the narrow issue of the EU; but this soon develops into a wider distrust of the masses.

To get around the awkward lack of enthusiasm for their project evinced by ordinary citizens, Euro-elites have developed a version of what Friedrich Engels called 'false consciousness'. Marxists used to contend that, if only the workers were in full possession of the facts, and free rationally to advance their own interests, they would vote for socialist parties. But in practice they were led astray by bourgeois interests. It was therefore necessary for good Communists to act in the real, rather than the stated, interests of the majority.

How often one hears that argument, *mutatis mutandis*, in Brussels. If only people weren't hoodwinked by Eurosceptic media barons, if only they weren't lied to by tabloids, if only they weren't whipped up by unscrupulous nationalists, if only there could be an informed and dispassionate election campaign – *then* they would surely see that deeper integration was in their interests. But because people are unable to make an unclouded judgement, Eurocrats are entitled – obliged, indeed – to disregard their superficial desires in pursuit of their true preferences. In his final interview as prime minister, Tony Blair offered a startlingly frank summary of the false consciousness theory:

> The British people are sensible enough to know that, even if they have a certain prejudice about Europe, they don't expect their government necessarily to share it or act upon it.[3]

Got that? We don't want our politicians to do as we say; we want them to second-guess our innermost, unarticulated desires. It need hardly be added that, from the point of view of the politician, this is a remarkably convenient theory.

Not all Eurocrats are cynics, of course. There are some idealists within the system: committed Euro-federalists who believe that it is possible to democratise the EU without destroying it. Their ideal is a pan-European democracy, based on a more powerful European Parliament. The scheme has been set out many times. The European Commission would become the Cabinet; the Council of Ministers would become the *Bundesrat* or Upper House, representing the nation-states; and the European Parliament would become the main legislative body. These were, indeed, the three specific proposals, put forward by Jacques Delors in 1990, that prompted Margaret Thatcher's famous response: 'No! No! No!'

Give MEPs more power, runs the theory, and people will take them more seriously. A higher calibre of candidate will stand, and turnout will rise.

Pan-European political parties will contest the elections on common and binding manifestos. People will add a European dimension to their political identity. It will, at this stage, no longer be necessary for Eurocrats to swat aside referendum results or impose policies without popular consent, because European democracy will have become a reality.

The problem with this idea is that it has already been tried, and has demonstrably failed. That failure can be inferred empirically from the turnout figures:

TURNOUT AT EUROPEAN ELECTIONS		
1979	(nine members)	62.0%
1984	(ten members)	59.0%
1989	(twelve members)	58.4%
1994	(twelve members)	56.7%
1999	(fifteen members)	49.5%
2004	(twenty-five members)	45.6%
2009	(twenty-seven members)	43.1%

Of those Europeans who had taken the trouble to register to vote before the June 2009 elections to the European Parliament, no fewer than 57 per cent declined to cast their ballots on the day. The figure is all the more remarkable when we consider that voting is compulsory in some member states, that others sought to boost participation by holding municipal elections on the same day, and that Brussels had spent hundreds of millions of euros on a campaign to encourage turnout. (One of its gimmicks was to send a ballot box into orbit, which critics joyfully seized upon as the perfect symbol of the EU's remoteness.)

Not that the abstention rate should have surprised anyone. There has been, as we can see, an unbroken decline in turnout since the first elections to the European Parliament were held in 1979. Still, the statistics are a serious embarrassment for Euro-integrationists. In the early days, they used to argue that the high abstention rate was a consequence of unfamiliarity, a function of the relative powerlessness of the new institution.

That theory has now been comprehensively disproved. Over the past 30 years, the European Parliament – like the EU in general – has been steadily agglomerating powers. Yet people have responded by refusing to sanction it with their votes. Back in 1979, when no one really knew what the European Parliament was, and Euro-elections were treated as series of miniature referendums on national governments, turnout was disappointing rather than disastrous. The more familiar people have become with the EU, the further it has fallen.

MEPs, naturally enough, respond to each new low by, in effect, blaming the electorate. They demand better information campaigns, more extensive (and expensive) propaganda. Europe, they declare, matters more than ever, and voters must be made to see it! It never occurs to them to infer any loss of legitimacy from the turnout figures, nor to devolve powers to a level of government that continues to enjoy democratic support. It is hard not to think of Bertolt Brecht's eerie lines: 'Wouldn't it therefore be easier to dissolve the people and elect another in their place?'

It won't do, either, to claim that turnout is falling in every democracy. It isn't. In the US, for example, it is rising: from 51.3 per cent in 2000 to 56.7 per cent in 2004 to 61.4 per cent in 2008. Turnout at European elections is far lower than at national elections in the same countries, and is falling faster. Falling, we might add, for the most obvious of reasons: very few people think of themselves as Europeans in the same sense that they might think of themselves as Portuguese or Swedish. There is no pan-European public opinion, there are no pan-European media. You can't decree a successful democracy by bureaucratic fiat. You can't fabricate a common nationality.

So far, so familiar. The undemocratic nature of the Brussels institutions has been a Eurosceptic complaint from the beginning. What is rarely appreciated is the extent to which, as well as being undemocratic within its own structures, the EU tends also to subvert the *internal* democracy of its member nations.

41

Consider a few examples. Ireland used to have exemplary laws on the conduct of referendums, providing for equal airtime for both sides and the distribution of a leaflet with the 'Yes' and 'No' arguments to every household. When these rules produced a 'No' to the Nice treaty in 2001, they were revised so as to make it easier for the pro-EU forces to win a second referendum. That victory was duly secured, but a result was that *all* subsequent Irish referendums, not simply those to do with the EU, were fought on an unbalanced basis. The same is true of Croatia, which dropped the minimum threshold provisions in its referendum rules in order to ensure entry into the EU in 2011.

When the president of the Czech Republic, Václav Klaus, declared that he was reluctant to sign the Lisbon Treaty into law, he was threatened with impeachment. He duly climbed down and, with poor grace, scrawled his name across the Bill; but, again, think of the precedent. From now on, any Czech President might face impeachment, not for impropriety, malfeasance or mental incapacity, but for sticking to the promises that he had very clearly made in the run-up to his election.

I could fill a book with similar cases: again and again, national democracy is vitiated in order to sustain the requirements of European integration. Think of the way in which, in Britain, successive party leaders have had to abandon their pledges of a referendum on one aspect or another of the EU. All three parties promised such a vote during the last parliament; all three have since reneged. Each such betrayal, of course, damages them vis-à-vis the electorate; yet they are prepared to pay that price for the sake of Europe.

Borrowing a phrase from the title of one of C. S. Lewis's works of adult fiction, I think of the phenomenon as the EU's 'hideous strength'. The novel of that name tells of a diabolical plot that takes the guise of an apparently beneficent bureaucracy known as the National Institute for Co-ordinated Experiments (NICE). One by one, independent institutions find themselves subverted, bent to the will of the bureaucrats. In much the same way, national politicians repeatedly act against their personal, party and national interests for the sake of European integration.

British party leaders have got off lightly compared to their neighbours. When Ireland's referendum on the Lisbon Treaty was announced, the European establishment required the Taoiseach, Bertie Ahern, to stand aside lest the corruption allegations swirling around him destabilise the 'Yes' campaign. He was duly replaced with the most pro-EU member of his government, Brian Cowen. Cowen went on to lose anyway and then – in a move much applauded in Brussels – sided with the European Commission against his own electorate, demanding that people vote a second time. Once again, the EU got its way, in the sense that Ireland reversed its decision. But the price paid by Cowen's party was devastating. Until the second Lisbon referendum, Fianna Fáil had been the fixed point in Ireland's party system, the star around which other parties orbited. It had won – in the sense of getting more votes than anyone else – every election since 1932, typically securing between 40 and 50 per cent of all ballots cast. In the 2011 general election, its share of the vote went from 41.6 to 17.4 per cent, as voters turned against a government that had meekly agreed to the EU's loans-for-austerity deal, saddling them with the cost of propping up the entire European banking system and turning Ireland into a vassal state.

The distortion of Ireland's democracy was just the beginning. Far more aggressive projections of the EU's hideous strength were to follow. November 2011 witnessed Brussels-backed coups in two EU member states – bloodless and genteel coups, but coups nonetheless. In Greece and in Italy, elected prime ministers were toppled and replaced with Eurocrats – respectively a former vice-president of the European Central Bank, Lucas Papademos, and a former European Commissioner, Mario Monti.

The two premiers, George Papandreou in Greece and Silvio Berlusconi in Italy, had inadvertently stumbled into the path of the EU's combine harvester. Papandreou's mistake was to call for a referendum on Greece's austerity deal – a move which was to prompt purple, choking fury in Brussels where, as we have seen, the first rule is 'no referendums'.

Papandreou was not a Eurosceptic. On the contrary, he fervently wanted Greece to stay in the euro, and had planned to campaign for a 'Yes' vote. His sin, in the eyes of the Brussels establishment, was not to hold the wrong opinions, but to be too keen on democracy. Leninists had a term for party members who, though committed Bolsheviks, nonetheless behaved in a way which jeopardised the movement. They were called 'objectively counter-revolutionary'. Papandreou's reckless desire to consult the voters put him in this category. Four days later, he was out.

Berlusconi, too, got on the wrong side of the EU's hideous strength. His pronouncement that 'since the introduction of the euro, most Italians have become poorer' was factually true, but sealed his fate. At a meeting in Frankfurt's opera house, Nicolas Sarkozy, Angela Merkel, the prime minister of Luxembourg (who heads the euro group) and the leaders of the IMF and ECB decided that the Italian premier was an obstacle to their plan to keep the euro together. We can hardly call it a secret plot: at the Cannes summit a few days later, officials were proudly wearing badges proclaiming their membership of the 'Frankfort Group'. One such official happily declared: 'We're on our way to moving out Berlusconi.'[4] If this was a conspiracy, it was what H. G. Wells called 'an open conspiracy'. Sure enough, a few days later, Berlusconi was gone, his exit triggered by a combination of a sudden withdrawal of ECB support for Italian bonds, verbal attacks from other EU leaders and a rebellion from Europhile Italian MPs.

It is true, of course, that both Papandreou and Berlusconi were already unpopular for domestic reasons – just as Margaret Thatcher had been when EU leaders and Conservative Euro-enthusiasts brought her down in November 1990. Had they been at the height of their powers, they would not have been vulnerable. Nonetheless, to depose an incumbent head of government, even a wounded one, is no small thing. Silvio Berlusconi, in particular, had survived a series of blows that would have felled anyone else. He had weathered accusations of bribery, soliciting underage sex, tax fraud and mafia links. He had shrugged off the attentions of – by his own count – 789 prosecutors and magistrates. He had laughed off gaffes on electric-rail topics from Muslims to Nazis. But he could not withstand the EU.

With Papandreou and Berlusconi out of the way, Brussels was able to install technocratic juntas in their place. Neither Lucas Papademos nor Mario Monti had ever stood for public office in his life.

Mr Monti, indeed, managed to fill his Cabinet without appointing a single elected politician. Both men headed what were called 'national governments', but these administrations had been called into being solely to enforce programmes which their nations rejected. Both men derived their real mandates from their support in Brussels, and everyone knew it.

The most shocking aspect of the whole affair was that so few people were shocked. Two countries which, in living memory, had emerged from dictatorship were now suspending multi-party democracy. True, the outward forms of constitutionalism were observed: both new regimes were formally endorsed by parliamentary votes. Similar things could be said, though, by almost every tyrant in history, from Bonaparte onwards. The fact remained that these regimes existed for the narrow and explicit purpose of implementing policies that their peoples would throw out at a general election.

The Brussels system had been undemocratic from the start, but its hostility to the ballot box had always been disguised by the outward trappings of constitutional rule in its member nations. In 2011, that ceased to be true. Apparatchiks in Brussels now ruled directly through apparatchiks in Athens and Rome. The voters and their tribunes were cut out altogether. There was no longer any pretence.

Chapter 4

– Falling for the euro –

How did so many clever people get it so wrong? The flaws in the euro project are not just clear with hindsight; they were visible at the outset and were widely pointed out. It was never going to be possible to jam widely divergent economies into a single monetary policy. It was patently foolish to allow Italy and Greece to join with twice the permitted debt level. Yet, in every national parliament, in every central bank, in every university faculty, in every BBC editorial conference, there was a collective suspension of disbelief.

Why? What were supporters of the single currency thinking? If you listen carefully to what Euro-integrationists were saying at the time, you detect a subtext. It's not so much that they liked the euro, it's that they disliked the people who opposed it. Listen, for example to the then Lib Dem leader, Charles Kennedy, in 2002:

The euro, despite gloomy predictions from anti-Europeans, has proved to be a success. We cannot afford to be isolated from our biggest and closest trading partner any longer.[1]

Or to the chief of the Tory Europhiles, Ken Clarke:

Opponents of the euro have been disheartened as their predictions of chaos and disaster have failed to materialise. The reality of the euro has exposed the absurdity of many anti-European scares while increasing the public thirst for information. Public opinion is already changing as people can see the success of the new currency on the mainland.[2]

For such men, the issue was never really economic, or even political, but tribal. Having defined the question, in their own minds at least, as a *Kulturkampf* between sensible progressives and ignorant Blimps, they became more or less uninterested in the facts.

The extraordinary thing is that many Euro-enthusiasts are still at it, quite unabashed by how things have turned out. Here, for example, is the historian Norman Davies in the *Financial Times*, long after the consequences of the euro had become clear:

'How marvellous,' they chortle in the Tory clubs; 'the busy-bodies of Brussels are meeting their come-uppance. Greece will push French banks down the chute first; but German banks won't avoid it, and together they'll finish Italy off. With luck, Italy will suck Spain into the abyss; Portugal will follow Spain, and Ireland Portugal. Just think of it! Those Irish traitors from 1922 will get their deserts! Terrific!'

Then continental banks lock their doors and the cash machines dry up. Minestrone kitchens appear on the streets of Rome. Spanish bullrings house the destitute. The bridges of Paris fill with rough sleepers. Weeks and months pass free of money. Europeans relearn the art of barter. When the cash flow stutters back, machines distribute drachmas again, the franc nouvel and the peseta nueva. Yet Britain's latterday

Blimps will still not be satisfied. They hanker for the whole hog; before we pull up the drawbridge, they say, the EU itself must vanish.[3]

For what it's worth, I have yet to meet a British Euro-sceptic who is enjoying the economic turmoil on our doorstep. It is plainly in our interest that the euro-zone – which takes 40 per cent of our exports, and comprises our allies and friends – should flourish. That's precisely why we are alarmed at the readiness of Eurocrats to sacrifice their peoples' prosperity in order to to keep the euro together.

Not that Norman Davies is much interested in what Eurosceptics actually think. One of the oddi-ties of the whole debate is that commentators who are quick to spot prejudice in others when it comes to racism, sexism or xenophobia in others are quite unable to detect it in themselves when it comes to people who don't share their *Weltanschauung*.

The odd thing is that, in my experience, British Eurosceptics are likelier to have lived abroad and to speak foreign languages than integrationists. In the article quoted above, for example, Professor Davies makes an elementary howler when he writes of 'le franc nouvel' rather than 'le nouveau franc'. You'd think that, when upbraiding his opponents as chau-vinists, he'd bother to get his French right. But for him, the issue isn't really about feeling comfortable with other cultures; it's about self-image.

None of this would matter if it were simply an academic debate. The trouble is that the people running the EU refuse to learn anything from the failure of their project. Since the crisis began, they have pursued only one policy: bailout-and-borrow. When it doesn't work, they accelerate it.

For years, EU leaders have been conditioned to spend public money. The first instinct of a Eurocrat, in a crisis, is to reach for his wallet – or, rather to reach for *your* wallet, since EU officials are exempt from paying national taxation. Expanding their budgets, of course, is what bureaucracies do best. As Mark Twain observed, if all you have is a hammer, everything starts to look like a nail.

Even so, there is something perverse about sticking to a policy which is manifestly failing in its stated objectives. Every new bailout is hailed as the end of the crisis. Every one fails, leaving the markets as sceptical as before, but increasing the mountain of outstanding debt.

Why this mulish determination to stick with a strategy that is impoverishing Europe? Some supporters of the project have fallen back on a cure-would-be-worse-than-the-disease shtick. They no longer try to argue that the euro has brought benefits – two thirds of the citizens who use it believe it has made them poorer, according to Eurobarometer – insisting instead that leaving would be impractical.

To British ears, such claims are eerily familiar.

When it became clear that the Exchange Rate Mechanism, the euro's baleful predecessor, was wrecking our economy, the Establishment lined up to argue that, whatever the flaws in the system, we now had no option but to stick with it. Pulling out, declared John Major, would be 'the soft option, the inflationary option, the devaluer's option, a betrayal of the future of our country'.[4] In the event, of course, Britain's recovery began the day we left the ERM: 16 September 1992, four days after John Major's preposterous prediction.

It's true that returning to national currencies would involve certain practical difficulties, but none would be insurmountable. By definition, all the countries in the euro have recently managed such a changeover: that's how they joined in the first place. I don't remember any Eurocrats at that time droning on about the huge costs and complexities of having to replace your banknotes. And, indeed, the switch would be easier now than it was a decade ago, because more money is digitised, and banknotes represent a smaller proportion of the currency in circulation.

I recently asked a Slovakian economist how his country had managed the monetary transition when it divorced the Czech Republic. 'Very easily,' he replied. 'One Friday, after the markets had closed, the head of our central bank phoned round all the banks and told them that, over the weekend, someone from his office would come round with a stamp to put on all their banknotes, and that, until the new notes and coins came into production, those stamped notes would be Slovakia's legal tender. On the Monday morning, we had a new currency.'

It's a little more complicated than that, but only a little. Why, then, do EU leaders persist in ruining Europe? Why are they inflicting deflation, poverty and emigration on the Mediterranean states, and open-ended tax rises on the northern states?

Euro-apologists sometimes claim that Europe is suffering from a debt crisis, not a crisis of the single currency. Latvia, Hungary and Britain, they point out, did not join the euro, yet they, too, have suffered. This is true, but beside the point. There is no question that personal, corporate and government debts are too high throughout the West, not just in the eurozone. But it was monetary union which turned what ought to have been a containable problem into a global catastrophe.

Had Greece kept the drachma, it could not have run up the monstrous debts it had accumulated by 2010: the markets would have stepped in and imposed a corrective at least three years earlier.

When the collapse came, newspapers reached inevitably for headlines about a 'Greek tragedy'. The metaphor is, in fact, rather an apt one. Greece's hubris came during the eight years that followed the launch of the single currency, when the markets allowed themselves to be convinced that Greek and German debt were interchangeable. During this period, while Greece enjoyed a synthetic credit boom, her productivity lagged further and further behind Germany and the other core EU economies. Years of EU subsidy had already debilitated the Greek economy, as the best and brightest graduates of each generation forsook the private sector for the security of EU-funded posts. But only with monetary union did the competitiveness gap become unsustainable.

Nemesis came in 2009, when it dawned on creditors that the Greek government was a separate legal entity, that its debt was growing far faster than its economy, and that there was no prospect of that debt being repaid. Nemesis is not too strong a word. The Greek economy shrank by 13 per cent over the next two years, and unemployment rose to 20 per cent. People reverted to barter as bank accounts were emptied. There were reports in 2011 of well-dressed Athenians rummaging discreetly in bins, of farmers taking emergency food supplies to their urban cousins.

After the hubris and the nemesis, we expect the catharsis: the moment of purification and emotional renewal that comes at the end of the tragedy. In this instance, though, the catharsis was artificially stayed. Greece was not allowed to default cleanly on her liabilities, leave the euro and start exporting her way back to growth. Such a policy would not, of course, solve everything: there were no easy ways out for a country in Greece's situation. But it would at least hold out the hope of an eventual recovery. The two biggest sectors of the Greek economy are tourism and shipping, both of which would stand to gain considerably from a competitive devaluation.

Instead of taking this option, policy-makers in Brussels and in Athens insisted that there was simply a short-term liquidity problem and that the debt crisis could be solved by improved tax collection and public sector reforms. In the meantime, more loans were pressed on Athens: by the EU, by the IMF and by a consortium of eurozone states acting bilaterally. The debt crisis was evidently to be addressed with more debt.

No one, of course, believed that Athens would be able to meet its obligations in full. Its debts were growing while its economy was shrinking, making default a mathematical certainty. Why, then, did the EU not get the whole unpleasant business out of the way? Why did it insist on deferring the inevitable, thus making the eventual default much larger?

For two reasons. First, it used the time to shift liabilities from the private sector to the public. In 2010, overseas financial institutions owned 42 per cent of Greek debts, and foreign governments 26 per cent, the rest being owed domestically. Over the next two years, those figures became 12 per cent and 64 per cent respectively, as the EU and IMF snapped up Greek bonds.[5] In other words, yet again, banks were able to shuffle off their bad debts on to the taxpayer. (Or, as supporters of the policy would no doubt put it, governments intervened to sustain a fragile financial sector. Take your pick.)

Second, because all sides preferred, if possible, to keep Greece in the euro. Greek politicians and central bankers regarded their participation as confirmation of Greece's status as a modern European country. Brussels officials were reluctant to set the precedent that membership of the single currency might be temporary. Both sides were prepared to suffer considerable pain for the sake of European amalgamation. The euro, after all, had been a political project from the beginning. Had it been a primarily economic endeavour, Greece would never have joined in the first place. The rules had specified that, in order to qualify, participating member states needed a debt-to-GDP ratio below 60 per cent. Greece's debt, depending on precisely how we measure it, had been around 120 per cent of GDP. As we have seen, the EU was always, at its core, a political rather than an economic enterprise. Its purpose was to ensure peace through political amalgamation, not to make its participating nations wealthier. If forced to choose, most of its supporters would sacrifice prosperity for unity.

In May 2012, it emerged that Helmut Kohl, then the German Chancellor, had been explicitly warned against allowing Italy and Greece to join the single currency until their debt levels were addressed. He brushed such warnings aside, insisting that the political imperative of European unity trumped any statistical problems. His successor, Angela Merkel, takes the same line. As we saw in Chapter One, she urges her MPs to put up money for the bailout fund, not by making any economic case, but by telling them that the euro is a question of war and peace. Put like that, it is almost literally beyond argument. Small wonder that, if they see monetary union in such terms, Europe's leaders are prepared to pay any price to keep it together. Or perhaps 'pay' is the wrong verb since – this fact is rarely mentioned – employees of the EU are exempt from national taxation. It would be more accurate to say that they are prepared to *inflict* any price.

On their side, Greek politicians have given up trying to persuade their constituents that the euro has made or will make them better off: no one would believe them. Instead, they make a wider argument about Greece being at the European table.

When I debated the crisis with a socialist MEP on television in February 2012, I suggested that Greece wouldn't begin to recover until it decoupled, defaulted and devalued. The PASOK man stared at me in horror. But this wasn't about the economics, he spluttered. It was about the European ideal. Surely – *surely* – it would be unthinkable for the EU to go ahead without the country where democracy was born. That would be a calamity for Greece and for Europe![6]

No, I felt like saying, it would be a calamity for you personally. As an MEP, you are far better off than you were as a Greek minister. With your party now at 8 per cent in the opinion polls, you have no obvious route back to national politics. And it's hardly as though there are many private sector alternatives in Greece at the moment.

This is a problem common to every EU country: because Brussels has been kind to the politicians, they genuinely struggle to see that it isn't in the interests of their constituents. Yet, on any objective measure, Greece has been ruined by membership of the euro. Her travails have been made worse by the determination of her leaders to keep her there.

It is possible to argue, of course, that the euro exacerbated, rather than caused, Greece's woes. Even apologists for the euro generally accept, in private, that, as far as Greece is concerned, monetary union turned a crisis into a catastrophe. But, they maintain, the EU was not responsible for the spending splurges of successive Greek governments, nor for the imaginative accounting methods with which they disguised their deficits, nor for the culture of tax avoidance.

There is some force in these objections. They do not apply, however, to Ireland. Here the case is absolutely clear-cut. Ireland had been doing almost everything right in the run-up to the crash. She had applied the principle of the Laffer Curve, lowering tax *rates* so as to increase tax *revenue*. She was running a healthy surplus when the credit crunch hit.

Indeed, as Ireland's boom began to accelerate in the immediate aftermath of the launch of the euro, many could see where it would end. The ECB's policy of ultra-low interest rates forced Ireland to pursue a catastrophically *pro*-cyclical monetary policy, with real interest rates of minus 1 per cent between 1998 and 2007. The subsequent crash was utterly predictable – and widely predicted. In 1998, in a paper co-written with Mark Reckless, now the Conservative MP for Rochester and Strood, I made the following forecast:

The European Central Bank must set monetary policy according to the needs of the eurozone as a whole. An interest rate that is too high for the core members will be too low for the periphery. In reality, though, the core members are preponderant. In giving them the interest rate they need, the ECB can't help giving peripheral states a double-dose of what they don't need: low interest rates. The consequence will be an unsustainable credit boom in those states and, in due course, a commensurately painful crash.

The UK and Ireland would be especially badly affected by monetary union with the Continent. With regard to Ireland, which intends to join EMU at the outset, this is already becoming clear. Of all the EU member states, Ireland is easily the closest to the UK. Not only are the two states linked by trade, investment and labour mobility, but their economies are

similarly structured. The strains which EMU is already causing in Ireland should serve as a vivid warning to Britain.[7]

I can't claim unique powers of prophecy. As Ireland's
economy overheated, every analyst could see that interest rates needed to rise. But, of course, there *were*
no Irish interest rates any more. There was only a
pan-European rate. In retrospect, the ECB's monetary policy was arguably too loose even for the central European economies; what is beyond argument
is that it was disastrous for the peripheral states, in-
flating a massive bubble which burst in 2008.

That, though, was only the beginning of Ireland's woes. Having crashed the Irish economy, EU
leaders effectively saddled Dublin with the cost of
propping up the entire European banking system.
It was the EU's insistence on a bailout that hiked
Ireland's rate to borrow ten-year money from 6 to
9 per cent. To make sure that Dublin caved in, the
ECB then threatened to withdraw liquidity from
Irish banks.

Ireland was forced to accept the package on
ruinous terms. Her repayment obligations, com-
bined with the inability to devalue, condemned
Irish workers to a generation of deflation, debt and
emigration. At the same time, the United Kingdom,
until then Ireland's largest trading partner, enjoyed
a 20 per cent competitive devaluation at the Republic's expense. And, as if all this were not bad enough,

Ireland was obliged under the EU treaties to join the Greek bailout, borrowing even more money to send to Athens.

These facts are worth rehearsing at length, because they show quite how high a toll the euro has exacted from some of its participating economies.

What will happen next? There are, at the time of writing, three possibilities: an orderly break-up of the euro; a disorderly break-up; and carrying on as at present.

Of the three, the last is plainly the most costly. This is not to say, however, that it won't happen. It is possible to envisage a scenario in which Greece, and possibly some of the other weaker states, default on their outstanding debts while remaining within the monetary union. To take the pain of a default without the compensating gain of a devaluation would be the worst of all worlds; then again, if economic logic had prevailed at any stage, we wouldn't be where we are now.

Although the advantages to Greece of a cheaper currency seem obvious to the outside observer, few Hellenic leaders appear interested in exploiting them. The central bank, the newspapers and almost all the politicians, like the PASOK man I debated against on television, see the euro as a talisman: a guarantor that their country is European rather than Levantine.

In Brussels, likewise, there are plenty of officials who elevate politics over economics, and who are reluctant to set the precedent that any aspect of European integration can be reversed.

The markets deem it unlikely, but we cannot wholly discount the possibility of a devalued euro limping on, despite one or more sovereign defaults. These defaults would, of course, keep happening, yet the euro could survive, battered but intact, for years. There are exporters within the northern states for whom such an outcome is rather attractive: a break-up of the currency would end the artificially cheap exchange rate from which they have been benefiting.

Nor can we discount the option of an unplanned break-up, where one or another of the stricken countries simply turns, throws off the Brussels-imposed austerity regime, leaves the single currency and unilaterally introduces exchange controls. There would be immediate advantages to that country, but disadvantages to the European financial system. Several banks would be at risk of collapse, a new round of bailouts and nationalisations would be decreed, and the 2008 credit crunch would be repeated on a far larger scale.

This leaves the third option: an orderly unfastening. In 2011, a Conservative peer, Lord Wolfson, offered a £250,000 prize to any economist who could design a mechanism for a country to leave the euro without causing economic chaos. Hundreds of entrants were attracted and, in March 2012, five finalists were announced. From their submissions, it was quite clear that none of the mooted objections was insurmountable. There were difficulties, ranging from capital flight to the settling of debts, but each of these problems was remediable.

While the economics are straightforward, the politics are not. One option, for example, is for Germany and her satellite economies to withdraw and establish a new, hard currency among themselves, bequeathing the legal carcase of EMU to the peripheral states. The question of whether France would belong is, in itself, a strained one but, assuming it could be answered, the political implications would still be colossal. Once a substantial number of EU states ceased to be legally committed to monetary union – currently a status enjoyed only by Denmark and the United Kingdom – the dynamics of European integration would have changed utterly.

The single currency, after all, is now the chief driver of political assimilation. The merger of interest rates, exchange rates and, progressively, tax rates, creates, to all intents and purposes, a single finance ministry. As John Maynard Keynes wrote, in a different context, 'He who controls the currency controls the government.'

It would be odd if the euro members did not adopt among themselves many of the elements of amalgamation that are now being pursued at EU level. The stage would be set for a split between a core Europe of tightly integrated states – what the French call *le noyau dur* – and a much looser association of peripheral countries, perhaps expanded to include the present EFTA members, linked to the core by free trade and intergovernmental collaboration rather than common political structures. We shall explore this option a little further in the final chapter.

The euro was supposed to promote peace and amity among its participants. In reality, it has had the opposite effect. People are suffering in the downturn and are, quite understandably, blaming Brussels. Worse than that, they are blaming other countries, notably Germany. Greek protesters regularly burn German flags and portray Mrs Merkel with Nazi insignia. The German press, perfectly reasonably, asks why German taxpayers should be expected to give money to Greece when this is the thanks they get. The single currency, in short, has brought relations between those two states to their worst pass since the end of the Second World War.

So if the euro is bad for prosperity *and* bad for friendship among nations, what is it for? Why do the Brussels elites cling so obsessively to the project? There surely must be more to it than inertia.

To answer that question, we need to understand the change in the nature of the EU bureaucracy: the way in which a once idealistic, or at least ideological, project has now become a way for a great many people to make a handy living.

Chapter 5

– The tyranny of the status quo –

W hen preparing the document that became the European Constitution, and then the Lisbon Treaty, the EU authorities made a great show of 'consulting the people'. In 2003, 200 organisations, representing 'civil society', were invited to submit their suggestions on what the draft should contain. Interested in how these 200 bodies had been selected, I put down a written question asking which of them received grants from the EU. After some toing and froing, the answer eventually came back: all of them.

You see how the system works? The EU sets up and funds an interest group. That group duly demands that the EU seize more powers. The EU then announces that, in response to popular demand, it is extending its jurisdiction.

Virtually every field of activity has some approved, EU-sponsored pressure group to campaign for deeper integration: the European Union of Journalists, the European Women's Lobby, the European Cyclists' Federation. These are not independent associations which just happen to be in receipt of EU funds. They are, in most cases, creatures of the

European Commission, wholly dependent on Brussels for their existence.

Nor is the racket limited to pan-European bodies headquartered in Brussels. The EU has been active in subsidising established NGOs within the nation-states, too. It starts harmlessly enough, with one-off grants for specific projects. After a while, the NGO realises that it is worth investing in a 'Europe officer' whose job, in effect, is to secure bigger grants. As the subventions become permanent, more 'Europe officers' are hired. Soon, the handouts are taken for granted and factored into the organisation's budget. Once this stage is reached, the EU is in a position to call in favours.

One example will serve to illustrate what I'm talking about. When he introduced the Bill to ratify the Lisbon Treaty in 2007, the then Foreign Secretary, David Miliband, made a great song and dance about the fact that it wasn't just Labour Europhiles who backed the text. A whole range of NGOs, he told the House of Commons, had also come out in favour: 'The NSPCC has pledged its support, as have One World Action, Action Aid and Oxfam,' he said, looking pleased with himself. 'Environmental organisations support the treaty provisions on sustainable development and even the commission of bishops supports the treaty. This is a coalition, not of ideology, but integrity'.

Integrity? A few moments on the Internet revealed that every organisation he had cited was in receipt of EU subventions. Most of them, it turned out, had also received grants from the British government. Hardly surprising, then, that they should dutifully endorse a treaty supported by their paymasters.

What *was* surprising was the extent of their financial dependency. When Mr Miliband sat down, I fired off a written question asking the European Commission how much money it had paid these organisations. It turned out that, in the previous year, Action Aid, the NSPCC, One World Action and Oxfam had among them been given 43,051,542.95.

Just think about that sum for a moment. Can organisations in receipt of such colossal subsidies legitimately call themselves 'non-governmental'? Can they claim to be independent? Can they even describe themselves as charities – at least in the sense that we commonly understand the word?

Why should any of us want to give money to a body that is already forcibly expropriating us through the tax system, and then using part of the revenue to lobby the government?

The other body which Mr Miliband cited, the 'commission of bishops', was a little harder to identify, but patient Googling revealed that its full name was the 'Commission of Bishops' Conferences of the European Community'. Far from being an episcopal body that just happened to back closer union, it was a Brussels-based outfit whose purpose was 'to promote reflection, based on the [Roman Catholic] Church's social teaching, on the challenges facing a united Europe'. In other words, while seeking to give the impression of broad support for a new transfer of powers to Brussels, the British Foreign Secretary was reduced to citing a body whose sole purpose is to interact with EU institutions, and which would be out of business if the EU disappeared. The French call the phenomenon *déformation professionelle*: the tendency, perhaps subliminal, to form opinions according to the dictates of your professional self-interest.

These various client groups can even be dragged into arguments between different EU institutions. When, for example, the European Commission sought new Continent-wide rules on pesticides in 2007, it set up a front organisation called 'Pesticide Watch' – an amalgam of various EU-funded bodies – to push it in the direction it wanted. MEPs were then duly bombarded by emails from this campaign – presented, naturally, as missives from ordinary citizens.[1]

In much the same way, the Commission pays Friends of the Earth to urge it to take more powers in the field of climate change. It pays WWF to tell it to assume more control over environmental matters. It pays the European Trade Union Congress to demand more Brussels employment laws.

To summarise, the EU firehoses cash at its dependent NGOs, these organisations tell it what it wants to hear, and it then turns around and claims to have listened to The People. And here's the clever bit: millions are thereby drawn into the system, their livelihoods becoming dependent on the European project.

There are occasional grumbles, of course. Transparency campaigners sometimes complain about the influence of corporate lobbyists – and, of course, they are right. Oddly, though, they see a problem only on one side, refusing to acknowledge any parity between the green pressure groups and poverty campaigners on one side and the big business confederations on the other.

When the European Parliament voted in July 2011 on a Europe-wide reduction in carbon emissions, the then Environment Secretary, Chris Huhne, sanctimoniously ordered an investigation into the lobbying efforts of the energy companies. These companies had indeed been intruding aggressively into the debate: like all lobbyists, they had taken naturally to the EU system, grasping that it was designed by and for people like them. Far more energetic, though, had been the lobbying from their counterparts on the other side: Greenpeace, the WWF and Christian Aid.

The two sets of corporates are mirror images of each other. Both perceive that they can achieve far more in the Brussels institutions than they could vis-à-vis national parliaments, dependent as these legislatures are on public opinion.

Again, let me illustrate the attraction of the EU to special interests with a case study. Between 2007 and 2010, the EU proscribed several vitamin and mineral supplements and herbal remedies, and subjected others to a prohibitively expensive licensing regime. Opinions differ on the efficacy of alternative medicine, but no one tried to claim that the remedies in question were seriously deleterious to human health.

The reaction from consumers was immediate, negative and overwhelming. Some 20 million Europeans found that a harmless activity which they had pursued for years was being criminalised. I can't remember receiving so many letters and emails on any question in all my time in politics. It is hard to imagine national legislatures, subject to the same electoral pressures, voting for such a ban. So Brussels became the target.

The target for whom? It was no secret. The restrictions were pushed strenuously by big pharmaceutical corporations. They could easily afford the compliance costs; their smaller rivals could not. Many independent herbalists, who had been in the habit of concocting creams and potions from their gardens, went out of business, and the big companies gained a near-monopoly.

Whenever Brussels proposes some apparently unnecessary rules, ask yourself *cui bono*? Who stands to benefit? Nine times out of ten, you will find that there is a company, or a conglomeration, whose products happen to meet all the proposed specifications anyway, and which sees the EU as a way to export its costs to its rivals. Thus are businesses, as well as NGOs, drawn into the Euro-nexus. Thus are powerful and wealthy interest groups in every member state given a direct stake in the system.

The EU's strength is not to be found among the diminished ranks of true believers; not among the benign cranks who attend meetings of the European Movement or distribute leaflets for the Union of European Federalists. Nor, in truth, does it reside primarily among the officials directly on the Brussels payroll, either in the EU institutions or in its dozens of semi-detached executive bodies (the European Human Rights Agency, the European Space Agency, the European Police College and so on).

No, the real power of the EU is to be found in the wider corpus of interested parties: the businesses which are invested in the regulatory process; the consultants and contractors dependent on Brussels spending; the landowners receiving cheques from the CAP; the local councils with their EU departments; the seconded civil servants with remuneration terms beyond anything they could hope for in their home countries; the armies of lobbyists and professional associations; and, as we have seen, the charities and NGOs which, once they reach a certain size, almost always begin a financial relationship with the EU.

These are, of course, persuasive lobbies within their home countries. They tend to be made up of articulate professionals. No government lightly crosses them. Nor are politicians immune to financial blandishments. It is common for former ministers to end up in EU jobs of one kind or another. Even heads of government often aim for such positions: several former prime ministers have wound up in the European Commission (José Manuel Barroso, for example), in the European Parliament (Jean-Luc Dehaene, Silvio Berlusconi) or in the wider Eurocracy (John Bruton, the former Irish Taoseach, became the EU's Ambassador to Washington). Members of the European Parliament receive a far more attractive financial package than legislators in any of the EU's national assemblies – even Italy.

The politicians, though, are vastly outnumbered by the corporate interests that have grown up around the EU. Theirs is the tiny public face of a swollen European *nomenklatura*.

One has to be careful when using such words as *nomenklatura*, of course. The EU is not the Soviet Union. It doesn't take away our passports or throw us into gulags; and, while it doesn't pretend to be democratic in its own structures, it rests ultimately upon the consent of 27 democratic nations.

There is one sense, though, in which a parallel can be fairly drawn. The Communists who seized power in Central and Eastern Europe in the 1940s believed that the force of their ideology trumped any considerations of freedom, democracy or the rule of law. They saw Marxism-Leninism as both irrefutable and inexorable and, while they had no intention of allowing their doctrines to be rejected at the ballot box, many of them sincerely hoped that the suspension of democracy would be temporary. Once socialism had proved its superiority, once it had shown itself to be more economically efficient than capitalism as well as more just, it might be possible to move to a phased restoration of parliamentary rule.

Such reasoning was shaken by the Hungarian rising of 1956 and obliterated by the Prague Spring of 1968. After that date, the *apparatchiks* gave up trying to persuade their electorates. Instead of agreement, they demanded acquiescence; instead of conviction, consent. The dots and commas of *Das Kapital* became far less important than the maintenance of their place in society.

Something similar has happened to Eurocrats. In the early days, the Brussels institutions were dominated by true believers, convinced that, in burying nationalism, they were burying war. They, too, saw the lack of democracy as contingent: once the people saw the benefits of European integration, it would be possible to make the system more accountable. Their Prague Spring moment came in 2005, when 55 per cent of French voters and 62 per cent of Dutch voters rejected the European Constitution. The mood change in Brussels was immediate and palpable. One of my friends, a senior French Commission official, asked wretchedly: 'How can the voters have drifted so far away from me?' (It is human nature, I suppose, to place oneself at the centre of the universe.)

Since then, euro-*apparatchiks* have been defensive and tetchy. Like their Comecon counterparts in the 1980s, they have been more concerned with keeping their positions than with winning the argument, less interested in altering public opinion than in avoiding it. Before the 'No' votes, they tried to convince themselves that Euroscepticism was essentially a British phenomenon, with perhaps a tiny offshoot in Scandinavia. Now, they know that almost any electorate will reject the transfer of powers to Brussels.

It was the great economist Milton Friedman who first used the phrase 'the tyranny of the status quo'. I wonder whether anyone who hasn't worked in government can fully appreciate the brilliance of his aperçu. The tyranny of the status quo is not simply a matter of people's innate conservatism, or of our psychological tendency to measure any proposition against the benchmark of current practice. It also rests upon the bureaucratic inertia that grows up around whatever happens to be the established dispensation.

Ask yourself this. If Britain were not already a member of the European Union – if our fathers had had the sense to negotiate a Swiss-style free trade agreement instead – would either of the two main parties now be arguing that we ought to join?

To put the question is to answer it. Why, then, is there such a consensus within the Establishment (as opposed to the country at large) in favour of continued membership? Precisely because it represents the status quo. For a great many important people, this is not a question of democracy or sovereignty, but a question of mortgages and school fees.

There is, as Adam Smith observed, 'a deal of ruin in a nation'. Or in a union. Just as the *apparatchiks* of Central and Eastern Europe clung to power for decades after the discrediting of their ideology and the collapse of whatever popular support they had enjoyed, so their European equivalents are in no hurry to stand aside for a cause so trivial as public opinion. How, then, is reform possible?

Chapter 6

– Our own dream
and our own task –

Every nation joins the EU for its own reasons. The French saw an opportunity to enlarge their *gloire*, *rang* and *prestige* (none of those words, interestingly, has precisely the same meaning in English). The Italians were sick of a corrupt and discredited political class. The good burghers of the Low Countries had had enough of being dragged *à contre cœur* into wars between their larger neighbours. The former Communist states saw membership as an escape from Soviet domination.

The German case is especially interesting. As we have seen, for German politicians of Chancellor Merkel's generation, the European project is beyond argument: a question of war and peace. It is important to understand the nature of this conviction.

German opinion-formers refer frequently, but always elliptically, to the Second World War. They talk of the EU as a way to 'avoid the worst in our history', or an alternative to 'the demons of the past'. In part, this indirectness is a way to avoid assertions which, if stated plainly, would sound ridiculous. A German politician who announced baldly 'If we don't give lots of money to the Greek government, we might find ourselves invading Poland', would, of course, be laughed at.

There is no question, though, that the sentiment is sincere and, in its own terms, wholly honourable. It is deeply offensive to characterise the EU as a German racket. One hears the charge all over Europe: from Frenchmen, from Dutchmen, from Danes, Poles, Serbs, Czechs, Greeks and, indeed, from Britons. In fact, Germany has never pressed her claims within the EU. She has been the largest net budgetary contributor from the beginning, yet is the most under-represented state, in population terms, in the Brussels institutions. German taxpayers have uncomplainingly handed over a larger sum through the EU budget than ever their grandparents did under the Versailles reparation clauses, and have asked for no leadership role in return.

Their reticence is not simply a question of guilt or historical responsibility. Europe has also, in the eyes of many Germans, solved a national problem that had existed for hundreds of years.

A. J. P. Taylor, with the aggressive anti-Teutonic prejudice that animated many Leftists of his generation, defined the German question starkly. There were, he wrote, simply too many Germans. Such a numerous, disciplined and industrious people would, if fairly treated, inevitably dominate Europe. Their neighbours had therefore, over the years, found various ways to treat them unfairly – that is, to prevent them from fulfilling their national aspiration and living together in a single state. Since the Treaty of Westphalia, if not earlier, European coalitions had conspired to separate the German-speaking peoples – into fragmented princedoms, into separate Hohenzollern and Habsburg realms, into the FDR and DDR. This habit, A. J. P. Taylor concluded, naturally made Germans resent their treatment, and so made the region inherently unstable.

European integration seemed to offer the solution. Here, at last, was a way for Germany to be united and prosperous without threatening anyone. As long as neighbouring states felt that Germany was, in some sense, their country too, as long as they felt a stake in her success, they would not resent her numerical or industrial preponderance.

In 1990, Helmut Kohl declared 'European unity and German unity are two sides of the same coin.' That sentence makes little sense except in the context just described. What the Chancellor was telling his countrymen was that, by creating a united European polity, he and his fellow leaders would also create a dispensation in which a united Germany would be accepted by her former enemies.

It would be churlish not to acknowledge the appeal of this argument, especially to those who grew up immediately after the Second World War. Germany in 1945 was ravaged and dishonoured. Her infrastructure had been bombed to wreckage, her reserves were exhausted, her people were hungry, she had again been partitioned, and there were foreign armies garrisoned on her soil. Had an aspirant politician clambered onto some clump of bricks by the ruined Reichstag and prophesied that, within fifteen years, Germans would be the most prosperous people in Europe, that they would be valued NATO allies, that they would have the economic leadership of the Continent and that none of their neighbours would resent or fear their recovery, he would have sounded like a madman. For Germans over a certain age, Europe was the totem that effected this magical transformation. No wonder it is beyond criticism.

Germany is, perhaps, an extreme case. But one thing that is common to almost all EU members is that they joined out of a sense of pessimism. Confident and prosperous nations, such as Norway and Switzerland, see no need to abandon their present liberties. Less happy nations seek accession out of, if not despair, precisely, then a sense of national angst. Sweden joined immediately after a banking collapse. Iceland registered a pro-EU majority for five bleak months following the meltdown of her financial sector; the polls swung back as the immediate crisis passed.

Britain joined at what was, on most measures, her lowest moment as a modern nation. Between 1945 and 1973 – the year she became a member – Britain had been comprehensively outperformed by every Western European economy outside Iberia. In retrospect, we can see that a great deal of this decline had to do with the war debt: Britain had amassed colossal liabilities during the struggle against Hitler and, for the next three decades, this debt was a drag on growth. Successive governments chose to inflate their way out of trouble which, of course, had a knock-on effect on productivity. By the 1970s, decline seemed irremediable. Britain suffered from double-digit inflation, constant strikes, the three-day week, power cuts and prices and incomes policies. It was during this black period that Parliament passed the 1972 European Communities Act, a decision confirmed in Britain's first national referendum in June 1975, which resulted in a two-to-one 'Yes' vote. It is hard to imagine a similar outcome had that referendum been held either ten years earlier or ten years later; the necessary sense of national pessimism would have been lacking.

It is worth noting, as an aside, that Britain's timing could hardly have been worse. Western Europe had indeed grown spectacularly between 1945 and 1973. Part of this growth was a bounce back from the artificial low of the Second World War. Infrastructure had been destroyed, but an educated and industrious workforce remained in place. There was also a mass movement of people, from the countryside to cities, from the Mediterranean to the coalfields of northern countries, and from former colonies to Europe. Europe, moreover, profited from massive external assistance. Thirteen billion dollars were disbursed under Marshall Aid, coming on top of the $12 billion separately contributed by the US between 1948 and 1952. Arguably even more valuable was the US defence guarantee, which allowed European governments to divert military spending to civil projects.

Sadly, from Britain's point of view, this relative growth came to a halt shortly after she joined. Western Europe lost its lead during the 1974 oil crisis, and never really recovered. In 1973, the year of Britain's accession, Western Europe – defined for these purposes as the fifteen members of the EU prior to the admission of the former Communist countries in 2004 – accounted for 38 per cent of world GDP. In 2010, that figure was 24 per cent. In 2020, it will be 15 per cent.[1]

Far from joining a growing and prosperous free trade area, the United Kingdom confined herself in a cramped and declining customs union. And, in doing so, she stood aside from her natural hinterland: the markets of the Commonwealth and the wider Anglosphere, which have continued to grow impressively as Europe has dwindled. It is hard not to think of the lament of the Prussian general when he first saw Austro-Hungarian troops in action in 1914: 'We have shackled ourselves to a corpse.'

Share of world GDP

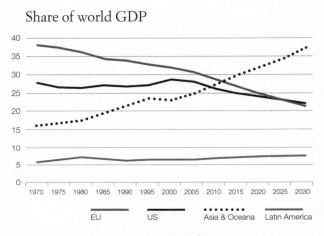

| 1970 | 1975 | 1980 | 1985 | 1990 | 1995 | 2000 | 2005 | 2010 | 2015 | 2020 | 2025 | 2030 |

EU   US   Asia & Oceana   Latin America

Source: Economic Research Service of the U.S. Department
of Agriculture, *International Macroeconomic Data Set*

Every country had her own motive for being involved with the European endeavour, but Britain was nonetheless in a separate category. Her initial assumptions about democracy, sovereignty and the role of the nation-state differed fundamentally from those of the other members. She was the only European country to have fought in the Second World War without, at one time or another, losing. In consequence, she did not begin in 1945 with a sense that her political institutions had failed. She did not, as many European states did, rewrite her constitution, so as to start afresh. And, of course, she did not share in the belief that patriotism was a dangerous and undesirable force. Across much of the Continent, self-proclaimed patriots had been tainted by their association with fascism. In Britain, by contrast, national loyalties had been the focus of resistance against the Nazi tyranny.

Britain was different in another important way. While she was connected by geography to Europe, she was pulled by habit and history, by language and law, towards more distant continents. This was, indeed, General de Gaulle's reason for vetoing Britain's first two applications to the EEC. As the general explained, when justifying his '*non*', if forced to choose, the British would always opt for what he called '*le grand large*': the open main. Perhaps he had a finer appreciation for the instincts of the British people than had their contemporary leaders.

Twenty-five years later, Margaret Thatcher was to make the same argument as the General, albeit less diplomatically, when she observed that, throughout her life, Britain's problems had come from Europe, and the solutions from the rest of the English-speaking world.

Hers was certainly a widely held belief in the 1940s. More than a hundred million men from the Empire and Commonwealth had volunteered to serve in the two wars. Alliance in adversity had created a sentimental bond which was strengthened by family connections. At first, these links came from emigration. Later, they were to come from immigration, too. Britain might be just 22 miles from the Continent, but her airmail letters and, later, her international telephone calls went overwhelmingly to North America, the Caribbean, the Indian sub-continent, Australia and New Zealand.

It was not surprising that Britain had little enthusiasm for a project that involved the creation of an internal European market at the expense of global commercial links. Britain conducted a far higher proportion of her trade with non-European states than did any other member. She still does. In 2010, the EU took 46 per cent of British exports – a figure artificially inflated by what economists call 'the Rotterdam Effect', meaning the shipping of goods through Antwerp and Rotterdam which are destined for non-EU markets, but which show up in the raw statistics as exports to the EU. For Belgium, the equivalent figure is 72 per cent.

It is nonetheless a myth that Britain was arrogant or stand-offish when the first moves were made towards European integration. Britain was deeply involved with, and committed to, the recovery of Western Europe after 1945. The Attlee government voluntarily passed 25 per cent of its Marshall Aid money to Germany, which was close to starvation. Britain was an enthusiastic – arguably the most enthusiastic – supporter of NATO and the Council of Europe, both founded in 1949.

It was not European collaboration that Britain objected to; quite the contrary. Her objection, rather, was to the particular model of integration favoured by the Euro-federalists. Throughout the early 1950s, Britain argued for the creation of a broad European free trade area, based on the 17-member Organisation for European Economic Cooperation – now the OECD. Such a body should, British diplomats proposed, remain closely linked to the United States and open to trade with the rest of the world. In particular, it should not artificially drive up the cost of food by creating a protected European farming sector, with prices regulated by the state.

These proposals, of course, served to spur the federalist countries into pushing ahead more quickly. Fearing the prospect of dilution, they determined on a small, tight community, based on a common external tariff, industrial and agrarian support and common political institutions. It is often said that these things happened only as a consequence of Britain having absented herself from the negotiations. Had the UK joined at the start, the Europhile narrative goes, Europe might have developed in a far more flexible and free-trading direction.

This version of events depends upon averting our gaze from much of what actually took place. Britain *was* involved in the discussions: her plan for a broad European free trade area, while it found no support in the old Carolingian states, was backed by the Scandinavian countries as well as by her old ally Portugal. In 1955 at the Messina Conference, Britain made one last attempt to divert Europe onto a more liberal path, arguing for a common market based on mutual product recognition, rather than a customs union based on uniform standards. (The British proposal was known, in the diplomatic jargon of the time, as 'Plan G'.) The federalist countries responded by agreeing a scheme that might have been specifically designed to keep the British out. Their tariff walls were especially prejudicial to Britain, which was in the habit of importing its food and raw commodities from the Commonwealth. The political institutions were especially alien to Britain's Westminster traditions. When the Common Agricultural Policy was agreed in 1960, it was based around supporting the smallholdings common in France and Bavaria. For Britain, a net food importer with relatively large and efficient farms, it would plainly be disastrous.[2]

No British government could join on such terms. Yet the Treaty of Rome did not end the discussions. Britain continued to negotiate with the Six, applying for membership five years later under Harold Macmillan, and again seven years after that under Harold Wilson. Both times, the negotiations broke down over the issues that had precluded Britain's involvement in the first place: access for Commonwealth exports, political union and the Common Agricultural Policy.

It was at this stage that Edward Heath, perhaps the most uncritical Euro-integrationist ever to have sat in Parliament, became leader of the Conservative Party and in 1970, much to the country's surprise, prime minister. Heath, who had been the chief negotiator during Macmillan's unsuccessful membership bid, was determined to get in on any terms. His fanaticism marked him out even from the other Europhiles on the Tory front bench: Iain Macleod, Reginald Maudling, R. A. Butler.

It is hard to imagine any other politician being prepared to sacrifice so much in order to join. Heath acquiesced in full to the EU's agricultural and industrial policies, its external protectionism and its anti-Americanism. He not only accepted, but loudly applauded, its ambition to become a single federal state. So abject was his attitude that, in the hours before joining, he handed away Britain's fishing grounds as a sort of late entry fee. Under maritime law, 70 per cent of the fish stocks in the North Sea were in British territorial waters. Under the Common Fisheries Policy, Britain was allocated a quota equivalent to 25 per cent by volume or 15 per cent by value. Indeed, Heath was even content to accept that the EU should carry on using its existing four official languages, French, German, Italian and Dutch. It was only at the insistence of Irish negotiators that English, too, was included.

It seems clear that Britain could have joined on such terms at any time. The metaphors about missing trains and boats and buses themselves all miss the point. To argue that the EU might have developed in a less federalist and less *dirigiste* way had the United Kingdom been present from the start is to beg the question. It was precisely because the authors of the project were determined on these goals that Britain was excluded.

In the circumstances, it was inevitable that the British people would have a different approach to European integration. The British authorities never tried to sell the project to their electorate as being primarily about peace. Instead, they appealed to the free-trading instincts of a merchant nation. The EU was rechristened the 'Common Market'. Membership was advanced as a wholly economic proposition. Even Edward Heath, the most committed Euro-federalist of his era, had the sense to downplay the political aspirations of the other states. His nickname, the Grocer, came from his tendency to read out price lists, seeking to demonstrate that essential household goods were cheaper on the Continent than in Britain. The implications for sovereignty were not simply minimised; they were expressly denied. In a television broadcast to mark Britain's formal accession to the EEC in 1973, the Prime Minister declared:

There are some in this country who fear that in going into Europe we shall in some way sacrifice independence and sovereignty. These fears, I need hardly say, are completely unjustified.[3]

That statement has been thrown back at the Conservative Party ever since. People felt, with reason, that they had been deceived by their leaders, that they had joined on a false premise. Instead of becoming members of what they had assumed to be a common market, based on the free circulation of goods and mutual recognition of products, they had joined a quasi-state which was in the process of acquiring all the trappings of nationhood: a parliament, a currency, a legal system, a president, a diplomatic service, a passport, a driving licence, a national anthem, a foreign minister, a national day, a flag.

At the same time, the common market itself never properly materialised. As we have seen, the European Commission was keener on standardisation than on mutual product recognition. Rather than ruling that if, say, a bottle of mineral water was legal in Britain, it might also be legally sold in Italy, and vice versa, the EU tended to lay down precise specifications: that the bottle should have a volume of not less than X and not more than Y, that certain minerals had to be included and certain others excluded and so on. Manufacturers and retailers who had no export trade – and the majority of firms do business within a ten-mile radius of where they are sited – might nonetheless find their product prohibited. Instead of expanding consumer choice, the European authorities were restricting it.

We can say with some certainty that the costs of regulation in the EU outweigh the benefits of the single market. The reason we can be sure is that we have the figures from the European Commission itself. The Commission tells us that the single market boosts the EU's GDP by 120 billion euros a year. We might cavil at this figure, of course: the Commission is hardly a disinterested assessor; it has every reason to talk up the numbers. Nonetheless, let us be generous and allow, for the sake of argument, that that figure is accurate. In November 2004, the then Internal Market Commissioner, Guenther Verheugen, asked his department to assess the total cost of business regulation in the EU. The answer? Six hundred billion euros a year. Thus, by the Commission's own admission, the economic costs of the EU outweigh the benefits fivefold.[4]

Britain was not the only state to have joined for largely economic reasons. Ireland and Denmark joined on the same day, largely as a consequence of British accession. Sweden, too, saw membership as being essentially about market access. In all of these countries, the mood turned as the promised benefits failed to materialise.

It was Britain, though, where the reaction was strongest. This was partly because the cost-benefit analysis was more clearly negative for the UK than for any other state. Britain has paid more into the EU budget than she has received back in 37 out of

38 years of membership (the exception being 1975, the year of the referendum on withdrawal). Indeed, for most of those 38 years, there were only two net contributors: Britain and Germany.

Net contributions to the EU budget, 1987-2010

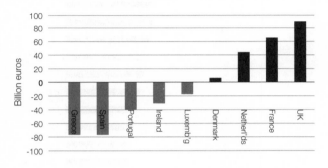

Source: Eurostat, European Commission and HM Treasury, *The Pink Book 2009, 2010* and *2011*

Britain was doubly penalised by the Common Agricultural Policy (see overleaf): as a net food importer with an efficient farming sector, she was hit both positively and negatively, paying more in and getting less back.

She was, of course, uniquely deleteriously impacted by the Common Fisheries which, for the next 30 years, did not apply to the Mediterranean or the Baltic, but only to the North Sea. It was, in other words, an overtly anti-British policy.

And, of course, her trade suffered. In 1973 Britain was wrenched from her natural trading

EU agriculture spending per capita

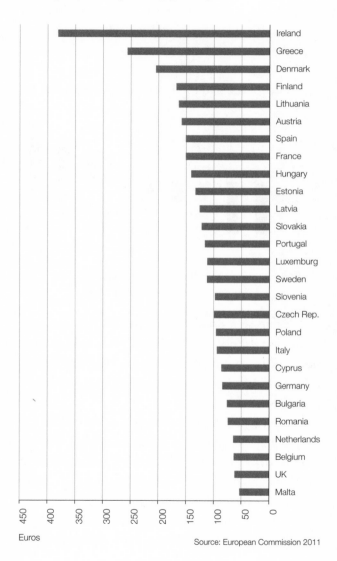

Euros

Source: European Commission 2011

hinterland. Until that year, she had imported food and raw materials from the Commonwealth, and exported finished products. At a stroke, Commonwealth free trade was replaced with the Common External Tariff. Trade was artificially redirected to the European continent. Glasgow, Bristol and, in particular, Liverpool were suddenly on the wrong side of the country, and their docks went into decline.

Britain had until then run a trade surplus with the existing EEC members, the Six. In 1973, that trade went into deficit, where it has remained to this day. Indeed, over the 38 years of her membership of the EU, Britain has run a cumulative trade surplus with every continent in the world except Europe. She has had to make up, through her exports to North America, South America, Africa, Asia and Australia, the current account deficit she runs with the EU.

The chief argument of the pro-marketeers during the 1975 referendum on continued membership was that the Commonwealth was finished, and that Europe was where the economic action was. On the most basic empirical test, that argument has been refuted. In 2012, the Commonwealth's economy overtook that of the eurozone. While Western Europe languishes in recession, the markets which Britain forsook in 1973 – Canada, Australia, New Zealand – are surging.

Look at these charts, compiled by World Economics using IMF data. The first two compare EU and Commonwealth growth rates since the year of Britain's accession.

Chart 1: EU

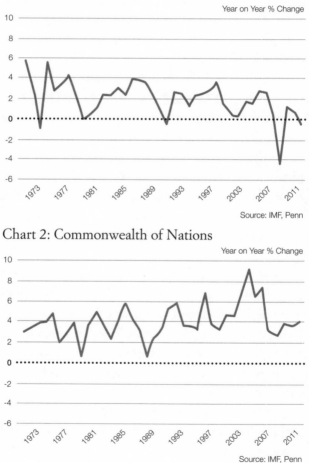

Year on Year % Change

Source: IMF, Penn

Chart 2: Commonwealth of Nations

Year on Year % Change

Source: IMF, Penn

The second two contrast the percentage of world GDP occupied by the Commonwealth and, respectively, the EEC Six and the eurozone. In all cases, the United Kingdom is excluded from the data.

Chart 3: EU & Commonwealth

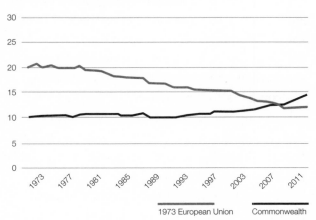

1973 European Union   Commonwealth

Chart 4: Eurozone & Commonwealth

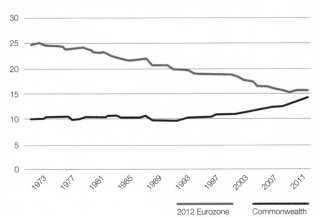

2012 Eurozone   Commonwealth

While the eurozone remains stagnant, the IMF expects the Commonwealth to grow at 7.2 per cent annually over the next five years. It is difficult, pondering these figures, not to conclude that, for four decades, Britain's economic policy has been based on a false presumption. Britain, perhaps more than any other member state, has alternative options. There is a world beyond the EU – a world whose opportunities cannot be fully exploited while Britain remains in a customs union as opposed to a free trade area.

The EU's Common External Tariff, by which Britain is bound, is, on average, between 5 and 9 per cent. For several of the member countries, this represents a historic low. But for Britain, it is a higher rate than prevailed a century ago.

Britain thus has a special interest in replacing her current terms of EU membership with a classical free trade area. But she is not alone. Several other maritime nations on Europe's edge also have a high percentage of non-European trade, and thus share Britain's interest in an orderly and amicable separation.

In September 2011, at a *Spectator* debate in London, I argued the merits of EU membership with the former Europe Minister, Denis MacShane. Denis came up with one of the more common, yet more puzzling, arguments for staying in. 'What you have to understand, Danny [he always calls me Danny for some reason], is that we sell more to Belgium than we do to the whole of India.' That, I replied, was precisely our problem. Which of those two markets represents the better long-term prospect?

This is not an argument peculiar to Britain. There has always been something curiously artificial about creating a single market in Europe at the expense of broader global commercial relationships. The whole point of a market, after all, is to swap on the back of differences. The more heterodox the market, the greater the benefits. Why, then, form a market exclusively out of similar industrialised European economies? And why, even more perversely, pressure other regions of the world into doing the same thing? Why, to pluck an example more or less at random, does the EU insist that the nations of Central America participate in their own regional trade bloc, complete with its supra-national parliament ('Parlacen')? Why does it refuse to sign trade or aid deals with individual states in the region unless they join this bloc? What possible advantage is there to the Central Americans in selling each other the products which they all produce: bananas, coffee, cut flowers?

The answer, of course, is that none of these initiatives is really about trade. All are about spreading the ideology of political integration as a desirable aim in itself.

What makes Britain unusual in the EU is not that it suffers especially badly from these policies. For a long time, it did, but the euro crisis has made it impossible to sell the EU as an economic proposition in any of the 27 states. No, what sets Britain apart is that the EU has only ever been presented here as an economic proposition. Unlike in, say, Germany, there is no reservoir of European sentiment to tap.

The United Kingdom has spent forty years conducting the fundamental argument about Europe which other states are only now beginning. Britain's institutions, temperament, size and experience equip it, as perhaps no other EU member, to seek a fundamentally different relationship with Brussels. Once it sets the precedent, however, others will surely follow, and Europe might yet be rescued from her current discontents.

'England will save herself by her exertions,' declared William Pitt in 1805, 'and will, as I trust, save Europe by her example.'

Chapter 7

– And we have not spoken yet –

W hat is the alternative to EU membership? We could do worse than to begin with some of the existing options. Several countries are part of the single market without being full members of the EU, ranging from the Channel Islands and Liechtenstein to Iceland and Turkey. While each has its own particular deal with Brussels, all have managed to negotiate unrestricted free trade while standing aside from the political institutions.

Consider, as an example, Switzerland. The Swiss rejected membership of the European Economic Area – intended as a precursor to full EU membership – in a referendum in December 1992. Although almost all the political parties had campaigned for a 'Yes' vote, they accepted the verdict, and set out to negotiate an alternative arrangement with the EU. Over the next three years, they negotiated a series of sectoral accords covering everything from fish farming to the permitted size of lorries on highways. More recently, they also signed up to the EU's passport-free area, the Schengen Accord, which the UK and Ireland have declined to join.

The result of these negotiations is that the Swiss

have all the advantages of commercial access without the costs of full membership. The issue has, in consequence, disappeared from the political agenda there. Switzerland participates fully in the four freedoms of the single market – free movement, that is, of goods, services, people and capital, but she is outside the Common Agricultural and Fisheries Policies and pays only a token contribution to the EU budget. It is true, of course, that Swiss exporters must meet EU standards when selling to the EU – just as they must meet Japanese standards when selling to Japan. But they are not obliged to apply every pettifogging Brussels directive to their domestic economy.

Critically, Switzerland is also free to sign trade accords with third countries, and often does so when she feels that the EU is being excessively protectionist. Britain, by contrast, is bound by the Common External Tariff, and is often prevented from adopting a more liberal position by the interest of a cosseted producer elsewhere in the EU. When the EU engages in bra wars with China or shoe wars with Vietnam, it is usually for the sake of protecting industries in Southern Europe. The United Kingdom is perforce drawn into these disputes; Switzerland is not.

Here, though, is the clinching statistic. In 2010 the Swiss exported four times as much per head to the EU as the British did. So much for the notion that our exports to the Continent depend on our participation in the EU's institutional structures.[1]

Might the other member states discriminate against our exports if we left? Hardly. We would still be covered by World Trade Organisation and, indeed, European Economic Area rules. More to the point, Britain's trade with the EU, which was in surplus before we joined, has been in deficit during 37 of the 38 subsequent years. In 2010, the last year for which full figures are available, Britain ran a deficit of £52.4 billion with the EU, but a surplus of £15.7 billion with the rest of the world.[2]

Our trade deficit is not in itself, of course, a reason to leave the EU. But it gives the lie to any notion that the other members would seek to restrict the cross-Channel commerce from which they are the chief beneficiaries. In any commercial transaction, the customer tends to have a stronger position than the salesman.

Britain should maintain her trade links with the Continent, her intergovernmental co-operation and her military alliance. We cannot but be interested in the affairs of our neighbours. At the same time, though, we should raise our eyes to more distant horizons and rediscover the global vocation that our fathers took for granted.

I have noticed, when debating this question over many years, that we often engage in a dialogue of the deaf. Supporters of the EU invariably conflate political participation with access to the European market. Many, indeed, seem genuinely to have convinced themselves that the two things are identical.

It is worth stressing that no one – *no one* – is suggesting that Britain should disengage from European trade. Withdrawal from the EU does not imply withdrawal from the European market. Indeed, under Article 50 of the Lisbon treaty, the EU is obligated to negotiate a commercial accord with any state that leaves.

Britain might choose to remain in the European Economic Area, like Norway. Norwegian exports to the EU in 2010 were twice as much per head as Britain's. Or it might prefer to leave the EEA, and rely on bilateral free-trade accords, like Switzerland. To repeat – for this fact cannot be repeated too often – Swiss exports to the EU in 2010 were *four times as much per head as Britain's*.

Some protest that, while this might be the legal position, an acrimonious split could leave the EU looking for ways to erect unofficial non-tariff barriers against British trade. Why on earth should it want to do so, though, when the balance of such trade is overwhelmingly to the advantage of Continental exporters? Over the past 40 years, Britain has run a cumulative trade surplus with every continent on the planet except Europe. Between 2005 and 2010, the EU accounted for 92 per cent of our total trade deficit.[3] It is hard to imagine that other

EU states would wish to prejudice their trade with what would be, by a long way, their single biggest export market.

As for the idea that we are too small to survive on our own, it rests on a misconception. We saw in Chapter One that the most prosperous people in the world tend to live in tiny countries. In the global wealth league table, the ten states with the highest GDP per capita all have populations below seven million. What matters to a modern economy is not its size, but its tax rate, its regulatory regime and its business climate. One of the reasons the EU's GDP is shrinking as a proportion of world GDP is that deeper integration means less competition among the member states, which in turn means higher taxes and more regulation.

Too small to survive? Britain is the seventh largest economy in the world, the fourth largest military power and the fourth largest exporter. It is a member of the G8 and one of five members of the UN Security Council. It enjoys close links to America and the Commonwealth (which, unlike the EU, is growing impressively). If seven million Swiss and four million Norwegians are able, not simply to survive outside the EU, but to enjoy arguably the highest living standards on Earth, surely sixty million Britons could manage.

British voters have worked this out for themselves: public opinion has turned against EU membership. Having been told that the EU is essential to their prosperity, they moved solidly against it once that argument lost its force. It has been more than ten years since any opinion poll offering a straight In/Out choice registered a pro-EU majority.

The odd thing is that, as the argument has moved on to economic territory, supporters of the EU have shifted their ground. It is not really about trade after all, they say. Rather, it is about having influence in the world.

All right, then. At the risk of stating the obvious, you have a more influential foreign policy when you have a foreign policy in the first place. Again, consider the EFTA states, Switzerland and Norway. The fact that Switzerland is not in the EU does not seem to have deterred the World Health Organisation, the International Olympics Committee, the International Labour Organisation, FIFA or hundreds of other global bodies from basing themselves on Swiss soil.

Norwegian diplomats are arguably the most proportionately influential in the world, having played a role in peace talks in Sudan, South-East Asia, Sri Lanka and Israel–Palestine. I remember talking to the Norwegian ambassador to London in 1994, just after his country had voted against EU membership. 'Before the referendum,' he told me, 'we were treated as a kind of extra EU state. I'd be invited everywhere with the other fourteen ambassadors, and often I wouldn't even get the chance to speak. Since the "No" vote, people have had to deal with me again.'

Britain has eight times the population of Switzerland and twelve times that of Norway. The idea that we maximise our influence by contracting it out to the EU institutions simply does not stand up.

What has perhaps changed most radically of all is technology. In the 1950s, regional blocs were all the rage. So, for that matter, were conglomerates of every sort: in business, in politics, in the trade union movement. Wise-sounding men asserted authoritatively that the world was dividing into blocs, and that it would be a foolish country that found itself left out.

Even as late as the 1970s, when Britain joined, this argument seemed plausible. Europe had embarked on economic integration and had, until that moment been doing rather well. People understandably, if incorrectly, attributed its growth to its amalgamation rather than to the factors discussed in the last chapter: large-scale migration, US assistance and, above all, the bounce-back from an artificial low in 1945.

Nowadays, though, distance has ceased to matter. Capital surges around the globe at the touch of a button. The Internet has brought the planet into a continuing real-time conversation. Geographical proximity has never mattered less.

A company in my constituency will as easily do business with a firm in Dunedin, on the opposite side of the planet, as with one in Dunkirk, 25 miles away. More easily, indeed. The New Zealand company, unlike the French one, will be English-speaking, will have similar accountancy practices and unwritten codes of business ethics. Should there be a misunderstanding or dispute, it will be arbitrated in a manner familiar to both parties. None of these things is true across the EU, despite half a century of harmonisation. Technological change is making the EU look like the 1950s hangover it is.

What would happen if the United Kingdom negotiated an amicable divorce? Britain itself, we can be reasonably certain, would be better off. But what would be the impact on the Continent? How many other nations might demand a similarly reformed relationship? By constantly focusing on the effects of EU withdrawal on Britain, we neglect the effects of British withdrawal on the EU. Britain would become, overnight, the EU's largest trading partner and most important neighbour. The European dynamic would be wholly altered.

Ireland and Denmark joined on the same day as the United Kingdom, and did so largely because of Britain's application. Thirteen years later, Portugal, too, joined her oldest ally. Sweden acceded twelve years after that and, while there were several factors at stake in her decision, it is hard to imagine that the issue would have been considered had the UK and Denmark not already been members. Something similar might be said another twelve years on of Estonia, Latvia and arguably Malta.

That's not to say that these countries would promptly reconsider their membership the moment Britain left. Whatever the original rationale of their applications, they are as subject to Friedman's 'tyranny of the status quo' as anyone else. In Copenhagen and in Tallinn, just as in London, a caste of well-remunerated Eurocrats is prepared to fight for its privileges.

Nonetheless, the removal of the United Kingdom would tilt the balance fundamentally in favour of the federalist states, above all the core, Carolingian countries and their satellites. Many of the more free-trading nations on the periphery would become uneasy. I don't think it is unreasonable to look forward to a separating-out: a division between a federalist core and a more commercial periphery.

Lord Owen, a former Labour foreign secretary who defected from that party in no small measure because of its hostility to the EEC, proposes precisely such a dispensation. Europe, he suggests, will divide into two entities, which he calls the European Union and the European Community. The former will contain the Carolingian core, along with Germany's economic satellites. It will have a single currency, a common finance ministry and the full panoply of fiscal union. The latter will contain Britain, Denmark, Sweden and some of the other merchant-minded coastal states. It will also include the existing EEA members, and probably the states currently negotiating with the EU; Serbia, Macedonia, Turkey and so on. The European Community will be linked to the European Union through the common nexus of a free market and through enhanced intergovernmental collaboration, but its members will remain politically independent.[4]

While we obviously can't be specific about which countries would be in which bloc, or the precise nature of the joint surveillance authorities they established to invigilate the common market, or about the nomenclature, some development along these lines is starting to look inevitable.

As we saw in Chapter Four, this separation might well be beginning anyway as a result of the euro crisis. The notion that all EU member states must accept a common outcome – *le finalité politique* in the jargon – has been overtaken by events. Membership of the euro, and of its associated rules on fiscal union, creates a political dynamic of its own. Various schemes for political combination, instead of being pursued in a desultory way by all members, will be embraced enthusiastically by some. The countries outside the euro will increasingly find that they are excluded from much else – to the horror of their professional diplomats, but the approval of their populations. There will come a moment when formally withdrawing from the EU's political structures – the European Commission and Parliament – and instead setting up EFTA-style joint authorities will seem a natural step.

Which countries are we talking about? The answer will of course depend on who is in power at the time in the various national capitals. We can though, point to certain states which, by their inclination and temper, tend to look out beyond the European continent.

At the start of his beautiful book *Voltaire's Coconuts*, the Anglo-Dutch writer Ian Buruma recalls finding an old guidebook in the Netherlands which had been published by the Wehrmacht during the German occupation. Among other things, it argued that, while the Eastern Dutch were proper Aryans who might eventually be assimilated into the Reich, the coastal Dutch were hopelessly mercantile, Anglophile and debased. Buruma agreed, albeit, obviously, from the opposite perspective. Indeed, he extended the argument to Europe as a whole, identifying Anglophile (and, by extension, Atlanticist) Europe as the free-trading littoral: the Hanseatic cities, Norway and Denmark, the Netherlands, Flanders, Portugal.[5]

These places have tended, over the years, to be sturdy and self-governing; to resent the power of distant kings; to value their civic privileges; to develop mechanisms of representative government; to favour open markets over state power. They have, in short, all the attributes that ought to make them Eurosceptic. Yet, until very recently, criticism of the Brussels system was more or less confined to the United Kingdom and the Nordic world.

Not any more. When 62 per cent of Dutch voters rejected the European constitution in 2005, something changed. The peoples of the hither parts of Europe are rubbing their eyes and shaking off the enchantment. Not all of them, obviously. But it's striking that Dutch and Scandinavian Europhiles are starting to adopt the same defensive tone as their British counterparts.

All that is needed is a catalyst. European integration rests, to a far greater degree than its supporters like to admit, on a sense of inexorability. People might not have chosen political union but, since it is happening anyway, they shrug and go along with it. Euro-integrationists often use the metaphor of a bicycle: if the EU isn't moving forward, they say, it will topple over (a ravening shark that must keep swimming or drown might be a more apt image). It is this fear that was behind the Euro-elites' determination to push ahead with treaty after treaty, despite the referendum results. The same angst lies behind their refusal to allow the stricken Mediterranean countries to leave the euro and start exporting their way back to growth.

If one of the four large member states were to

secede, that sense of inevitability would evaporate. Other countries, too, would seek a free-trade-plus relationship in place of full membership. In time, they might join the four EFTA countries, Iceland, Norway, Switzerland and Liechtenstein, to form an outer Europe, linked to the federalist states through the common bond of a European free trade zone.

In effecting such a change, Britain might reasonably hope to improve her relations with Continental states. The EU was designed as a peace project; but as integration has become tighter, it is causing animosities among its peoples. By withdrawing from the argument, Britain would remove the single greatest cause of her quarrels with nearby lands. The core, federalist countries would find, for their part, that they had lost a bad tenant and gained a good neighbour. Secession is now the greatest gift Britain could give Europe.

– Notes –

Chapter 1

1 Charles de Gaulle, *Mémoires d'Espoir: Le Renouveau*, 1970.
2 Kennedy popularised the theory, but acknowledged that it was first proposed by the Australian historian E. L. Jones in his 1987 study, *The European Miracle*.
3 Wilhelm Röpke, *A Humane Economy*, 1960.
4 *The World Factbook*, CIA, 2011.
5 Gibbon, *The History of the Decline and Fall of the Roman Empire*, 1776.
6 *Sunday Telegraph*, 15 May 2005. The Commissioner doctored her website to remove the offending words after they were publicised by this author.
7 John Laughland, *The Tainted Source: The Undemocratic Origins of the European Idea*, 1997.
8 Herman Van Rompuy, speech in Berlin, 9 November 2010.
9 Angela Merkel, speech to the Bundestag, 24 October 2011.
10 Macaulay, *The History of England from the Accession of James the Second*, 1848.
11 Antony Beevor, *Berlin: The Downfall 1945*, 2002.
12 Robert Wistricht, *Hitler and the Holocaust*, 2001.

Chapter 2

1 George Orwell, *Politics and the English Language*, 1946.
2 De Gaulle, press conference in London, 25 May 1942.
3 Max Weinrich, '*A shprakh iz a dialekt mit an armey un flot*', YIVO Bleter, 1945.
4 James VI & I, accession speech to Parliament, 1603.
5 Noel Malcolm, *Bosnia: A Short History*, 1993.

Chapter 3

1 José Manuel Durão Barroso, speech in Berlin, 9 November 2011.
2 *Daily Telegraph*, 17 July 2005.
3 *Guardian*, 26 April 2007.
4 *Spectator*, 12 November 2011.

Chapter 4

1 *Daily Telegraph*, 14 May 2002.
2 *The Times*, 15 May 2002.
3 *Financial Times*, 23 October 2011.
4 *The Times*, 11 September 1992.
5 Raoul Ruparel, *Open Europe*, 2011.
6 *The Record Europe*, BBC, 17 February 2012.
7 *The Euro: Bad for Business*, European Research Group, 1998.

Chapter 5

1 Chris Heaton-Harris, MEP, speech to the European Parliament, 27 October 2007.

Chapter 6

1 US Department of Agriculture, 2010.
2 Martin Schaad, *Contemporary European History*, 1998.
3 BBC broadcast, 2 January 1973.
4 *EU Competitiveness Report*, 5 November 2004.

Chapter 7

1 *The Economist*, 19 January 2012.
2 *The Pink Book*, HM Treasury, 2011.
3 *Global Britain, the EU and the Deficit*, 2011.
4 David Owen, *Europe Restructured*, 2012.
5 Ian Buruma, *Voltaire's Coconuts, or Anglomania in Europe*, 2000.